Shakespeare

HAMMOND®
INCORPORATED
MAPLEWOOD, NEW JERSEY 07040

THAMESIS FLVVI

Martin Fido

Shakespeare

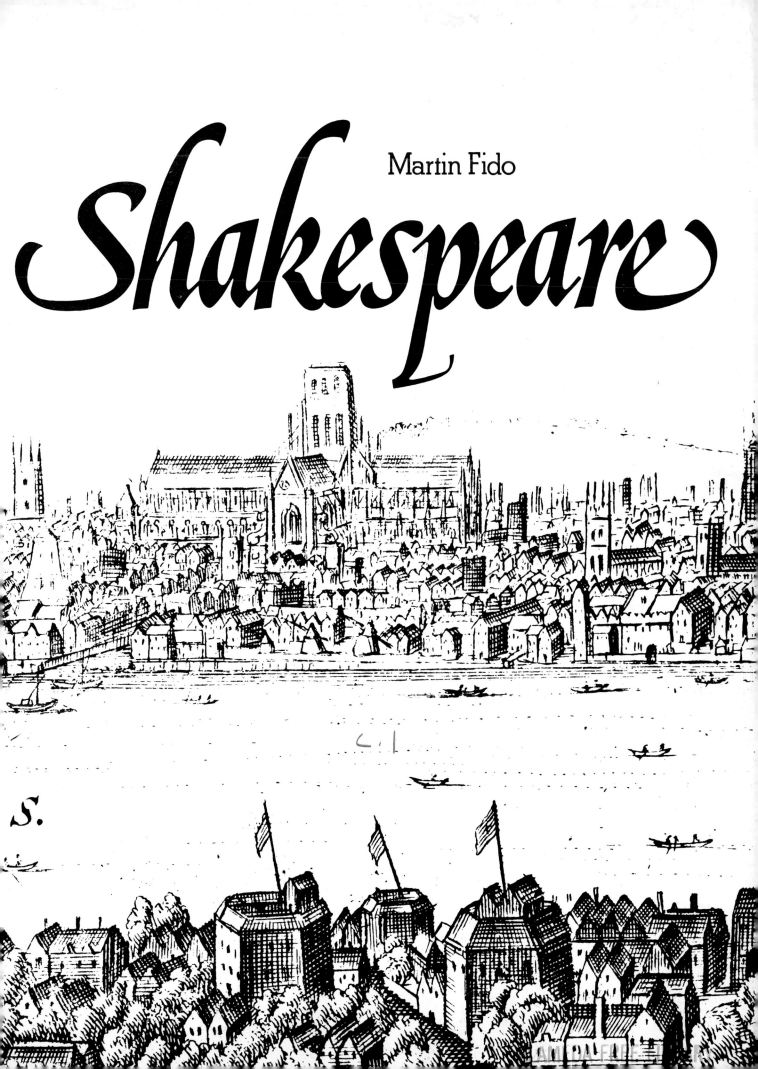

To
Rebecca, Abigail and Austin

&B
SHAKESPEARE, W.

Published in 1978 by
Hammond Incorporated,
Maplewood, New Jersey 07040

ISBN 0-8437-3130-3
Library of Congress Catalog Card number 78-53940

Printed in Spain by
Mateu Cromo Artes Gráficas S.A. Madrid
Phototypeset by Tradespools Ltd, Frome, Somerset

ACKNOWLEDGEMENTS

Generations of scholarly work on Shakespeare is lucidly and wittily summarised in Samuel Schoenbaum's *Shakespeare's Lives*. Indispensable to me, I would also recommend it to the reader who wants to pursue the trail of Shakespearean biography for a further thousand pages. It is as clear and entertaining as it is comprehensive and scholarly.

Schoenbaum's brief life of Shakespeare has not been available to me in working on this book, but his exposure of William Bott in *The Times Literary Supplement* during 1977 has been drawn upon.

As Schoenbaum observes, the popular biographer of Shakespeare inevitably draws his material from certain major sources. Sir Edmund Chambers' *William Shakespeare: a Study of Facts and Problems* is still the standard life of Shakespeare (though Schoenbaum's corpus of work is steadily moving towards superceding it) and gives transcriptions of a large number of documents. Edgar Fripp's *Shakespeare: Man and Artist* gives a vast amount of background information, especially in relation to Stratford local history, and I have leaned heavily on both of these. F. E. Halliday's *A Shakespeare Companion* is an essential tool for quick reference. Harley Granville Barker and G. B. Harrison's *Companion to Shakespeare Studies* is still more useful than the recent publication of *A New Companion* might *prima facie* suggest.

Andrew Gurr's *The Shakespearean Stage 1574–1642* does, as it claims, bring together the essentials from a mass of widely dispersed material. A. M. Nagler's *Shakespeare's Stage* is useful, and C. Walter Hodges' *The Globe Restored* and *Shakespeare's Second Globe* give the most widely respected account of the physical nature of Shakespeare's theatre. T. W. Baldwin's *The Organization and Personnel of the Shakespearean Company*, now fifty years old, has to be used with circumspection, but has not been comprehensively replaced.

The Riverside Shakespeare contains material that usefully summarizes the position in many fields of Shakespeare scholarship, and has the advantage over many volumes of the *New Arden Shakespeare* of having been very recently published. The better volumes of the *New Arden* (better from my present viewpoint meaning most useful in their introductory material) have not been slighted. I have found Andrew Cairncross's *Henry VI*, H. J. Oliver's *The Merry Wives of Windsor*, and Agnes Latham's superb *As You Like It* of peculiar value.

These are the books I have kept at my fingertips throughout the time of writing. Many others consulted and studied have either contributed to my general awareness of Shakespeare, or illuminated (or obfuscated) some single point. The great textual critics of the twentieth century have yielded almost nothing used in the explicit matter of this book, but had I never studied Greg, McKerrow, and Hinman I should have had far less sense of the conditions under which Shakespeare's plays became books, and the precise

kind of historical documents those books are. Work on the Elizabethan theatre by M. C. Bradbrook, Alfred Harbage, Enid Welsford and Una Ellis-Fermor has contributed to my mental picture of Shakespeare's working environment. Various numbers of the *Shakespeare Survey* have been consulted.

Some mention should be made of the more detailed investigators and discoverers. Leslie Hotson cannot be ignored. I have drawn on his *The Death of Christopher Marlowe* and *Shakespeare's Motley* with confidence; *Shakespeare Versus Shallow*, *Shakespeare's Sonnets Dated* and *Mr W. H.* either very guardedly or with stated reservations; *The First Night of Twelfth Night* and *Shakespeare's Wooden O* not at all, at least consciously. It must be observed that even when Hotson's main theses do not convince, his books invariably provide a wealth of fascinating background detail.

G. P. V. Akrigg's *Shakespeare and the Earl of Southampton* is the best book on its subject, and adds some facts to its chosen and explicit exploitation of speculation. A. L. Rowse's latest theories are to be found in his *Shakespeare the Elizabethan*: students interested in earlier phases of Rowsean revelation will find it in his lives of Shakespeare, Southampton and Forman, and his study of Shakespeare's sonnets.

I share Schoenman's admiration and respect for Marchette Chute's *Shakespeare of London*, which makes no claim to be a work of original scholarship, but organises very deftly a wide and well chosen range of material. I will not offend by naming the proponents of Catholic Shakespeares, deeper and darker Schools of Night and increasingly minor Rival Poets whose books and monographs I have read, pondered and disbelieved. With regret, too, I pass over the fine general studies of critical and linguistic approaches to Shakespeare which have helped to form my impression of his work. I made no special study of any critical writing for the purpose of this book. The passage cited from A. C. Bradley is from his *Shakespearean Tragedy*.

Finally, letters have shown me in the past that even scholarly writers finding no footnotes and a select list of acknowledgements may overlook the use of obvious scholarly tools. I have made use of the *Dictionary of National Biography* and the *Oxford Companion to English Literature* from time to time.

I am indebted to the staffs of the libraries of the University of the West Indies, Cave Hill, and the Bridgetown Public Library. I am also most grateful to Mrs E. M. Fido and Mrs C. R. Seymour for the loan of typewriters on which to make a fair copy of my foul papers.

Martin Fido
Barbados-Cornwall-Shropshire
1978

Contents

An Epistle to the Great Variety of Readers

YOU HAVE been sadly abused in the matter of Shakespeare. The majority of books offering you an introduction to his life and writings present specious theories as though they were established truth, and, all too often, special pleading as though it were sober history. Faced with unelucidated and contradictory assertions, you have been driven to suspect that there might be truth in the weird fantasies of those who propose that Bacon, or some other prominent Elizabethan might have written Shakespeare's plays.

So let us clear away that delusion immediately. The Baconian and similar 'theories' came into being when ill-judged critical adulation of Shakespeare had risen to such proportions that it seemed no mere mortal could have written such highly-praised works. Many of the early Baconians therefore proposed that a syndicate of the greatest names known to them must have collaborated to produce the works known as Shakespeare's. They were never able to produce the smallest shred of evidence that such a syndicate existed. Nor has anybody ever suggested a convincing reason for Bacon or anyone else to disclaim his own works and father them on to a leading actor of his day. Certainly a snobbish desire to foist the opus on to a more aristocratic author than the Stratford glover's son has been apparent in the writing of some of the pseudo-scholars. And some disappointment that the true scholars of the nineteenth century discovered facts about the poet's business life and not his intellectual life played its part, too.

No one with any real knowledge of Elizabethan and Jacobean history, or any real literary sensitivity, or any training in historical scholarship has ever believed for one instant that Shakespeare's plays were fraudulently passed off on the public over his name. No pseudo-scholar has ever explained the fact that people who knew him well–Robert Greene, Henry Chettle, Ben Jonson, John Hemmings, Henry Condell–all left printed testimony to their awareness that William Shakespeare the actor was William Shakespeare the author. Nobody left any testimony at all to any other suggestion.

Why, then, have you been so ill used that you have heard of these absurd theories, and yet may not be familiar with the known facts of Shakespeare's life? Principally because those facts are meagre, and not all particularly interesting, as is the case with most men, not of the governing class, who died three hundred years ago. We know far more about Shakespeare than we do about his contemporary Cyril Tourneur, about whom we know only that his name appeared on the title pages of two plays which were not very popular, and he once carried letters from the court to Brussels. On the other hand, we know far less about Shakespeare than we do about John Donne, whose connections with court circles mean that most of his career can be traced with certainty and many of his letters have survived.

Put briefly, we know when and where Shakespeare was born and died, and who his parents were. We know when and who he married, and when his children were born, married and died. We know when his writing first attracted printed notice, and that he was by then an actor. We know who he acted with, and quite a lot about the organisation of the theatre company he worked with. We know quite a lot about his business transactions in his home town. We know a little of the way his work was esteemed by contemporaries, and a very little about the way he worked as a writer. All these things *known* rest on solid documentation: entries in parish registers, legal documents, published observations on Shakespeare, and the like. These are the *facts*.

But facts may be bolstered by tradition. Sixty or seventy years after Shakespeare's death, antiquaries noticed that a great writer's life was in danger of being forgotten, and some of them collected any surviving rumours about him they could glean from Stratford-upon-Avon gossip, or actors' memories of what they had heard told. What they noted down passed into printed biographies of Shakespeare, and became traditional by repetition.

Such material is difficult to weigh. Some early traditions were later verified by the discovery of records: Nicholas Rowe in 1709 had no documentation to prove his statement that Shakespeare, while still young, married 'the daughter of one Hathaway'. But an entry in the Bishop of Worcester's Register proves it to be true in every detail. On the other hand some traditions have had a short life: such was the story John Aubrey picked up in Stratford in the late seventeenth century that Shakespeare was a butcher's son and used to make a grand speech whenever he killed a calf. Records at Stratford established that Shakespeare was not a butcher's son.

Since material collected from the same sort of popular recollection at the same sort of time has sometimes been proven true and sometimes false, we have to treat it with caution. Often it is more familiar than definite facts. You are more likely to have heard that Shakespeare poached deer in his youth (an unsubstantiated tradition) than that he helped persuade a head-dress maker's apprentice to marry his master's daughter (a fact, sworn to in court). But the treatment of traditions is one of the first ways in which you are likely to be abused. Often you have been given them as though they were facts: sometimes they have been suppressed almost entirely, on the unscholarly assumption that what is traditional must be inaccurate or untrue.

The most misleading information you have been offered as though factual has, however, been the inferences. An inference might be presented as a syllogism, one premiss usually being a fact known about Shakespeare and the other a matter of commonsense observation or general historical knowledge, from which a conclusion is inferred. It is obviously a reasonable proceeding, but it is dangerous to present the conclusions as facts. Here are two valid syllogistic inferences about Shakespeare's father:

> John Shakespeare made his mark on documents to which some of his colleagues signed their names.
> Men who sign with marks cannot (usually) write their names.
> Therefore John Shakespeare was (probably) illiterate.

But

> John Shakespeare was appointed Stratford Borough Chamberlain.
> Stratford's Chamberlains were (usually) literate men.
> Therefore John Shakespeare was (probably) literate.

You are entitled to be aware, then, that any inference drawn is not a fact. If the second premiss is no stronger than a likelihood, then the conclusion is no more than a supposition. And if the first is drawn from Shakespeare's writings, on the supposition that these must contain autobiographical elements, then the first premiss is itself suppositional.

The worst abuse to which you are commonly submitted is the presentation of inferences and suppositions built upon each other in long, apparently logical chains resting on premisses drawn from Shakespeare's works. Such speculation is akin to guessing. It is not true, in scholarly matters, that your guess is as good as mine. But it is equally not true that anyone's guess is entitled to be hailed as a fact or a discovery. A guess is a guess, and can only be more or less plausible, not more or less certain.

I have tried, in dealing with Shakespeare's life, to keep facts distinct from speculations and arguments. When I say, 'Shakespeare did so and so', this means that there is documented evidence that he did. When I think it probable that Shakespeare did so and so, I have said so. And when the legend built upon tradition has to be taken into account, I have identified what we are dealing with.

But one contentious area remains. We are looking at Shakespeare's writings as well as his doings, and it is solely because of them that anyone gives a hoot about the ownership of some land at Welcombe in 1613, or the market for knitted stockings at Evesham in 1598. Yet the assessment of Shakespeare's writings is in the last analysis a matter of opinion. If I don't let you know my opinions, you won't know why I think it worth my while to write and yours to read about Shakespeare. So I have given my opinions freely and without apology or identification, particularly in the chapters dealing with groups of plays. If you disagree, you are disagreeing with me. So if you don't agree that *Hamlet* is the kind of play I think it is, then cast an execration upon my head, and go back to reading Shakespeare. For as his friends and colleagues and first editors said in presenting their volume of his collected plays to the public,

> And if you do not like him, surely you are in some manifest danger, not to understand him. And so we leave you to other of his Friends, whom if you need can be your guides: if you need them not, you can lead yourselves and others. And such Readers we wish him.

I am,
Your worships'
most bounden,
Martin Fido.

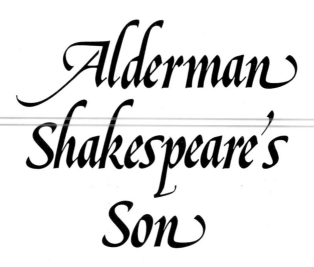

Alderman Shakespeare's Son

IN 1564 JOHN SHAKESPEARE was a rising man. Born about 1529, the son of a small tenant farmer in Snitterfield, near Stratford-upon-Avon, John became a successful glover occupying a comfortable house in Henley Street, Stratford, and owning another in Greenhill Street. He was one of the fourteen Capital Burgesses who, together with fourteen Aldermen, comprised the Corporation of Stratford under the chairmanship of a Bailiff. Perhaps most significant of all in an England which had been unalloyedly fuedal only a hundred years earlier, John Shakespeare had married the daughter of his father's former landlord. As a self-made bourgeois of peasant birth, he had contracted a connection with the petty gentry.

Mary Arden was the youngest daughter of Robert Arden, gentleman, of Wilmcote. He died in 1556 leaving Mary the estate of Asbies in Wilmcote, and the sum of £6.13s.6d. (six pounds, thirteen shillings and sixpence). Mary's money was left to her unconditionally. (Her stepmother received a similar sum on condition that she did not quarrel with another daughter, Alice!) Within a year of her father's death Mary Arden married John Shakespeare and took up residence in Henley Street.

John Shakespeare's first recorded appearance is dismal. In 1552 he was fined for having a dunghill in front of his house in Henley Street. Tudor England did not, of course, enjoy running water or municipal garbage clearance. Household refuse of all kinds had to be put on muckheaps, and the situation and size of these had to be controlled. We need not suspect John Shakespeare of committing any peculiarly nauseous offence.

But thereafter John's rise was steady. In 1556 he served as one of the borough's Tasters, responsible for inspecting bread and ale. A year after his marriage he served as Constable, responsible for maintaining law and order in the borough. Between 1561 and 1565 he was Chamberlain and Acting Chamberlain, responsible for the oversight and maintenance of Corporation property. And in 1564 his name appears for the first time in the list of Capital Burgesses, though he had probably been one for several years.

1564 was the year of Shakespeare the writer's birth. It was also the year in which Stratford Corporation co-opted a peculiarly unsavoury Alderman. This was William Bott, occupant of the splendid house, New Place. Bott was a cunning lawyer, who used a web of false promises and legal instruments to gain control over his

Examples of the gloves worn by wealthy people in the last years of the seventeenth century.

son-in-law's property. The locally powerful Clopton family accused him of having treated one of their scions in the same way, and darkest of all was the suspicion that he had poisoned his own daughter to ensure possession of her husband's property.

It was not, however, for these practices that Bott lost his Aldermanship a year after his appointment. In May 1565 he quarrelled with his colleagues and declared that, 'there was never an honest man of the council or the body of the corporation of Stratford'. Furious at this insult, the Corporation expelled Bott and nominated John Shakespeare in his place. Now the worthy glover was entitled to wear a furred gown on civic occasions, to take a front place in all local events, and to proceed in four years to become Bailiff (Mayor, in effect) of his town. The child William was by birthright a member of the prosperous provincial bourgeoisie.

On 26 April 1564, the baptism of 'Gulielmus filius Johannes Shakespeare' (William son of John Shakespeare) was entered in the register of Holy Trinity Church, Stratford. His birthday might have been any of the four or five preceding days. The popular tradition that identifies it with 23 April, St George's Day and the day Shakespeare died, is more patriotic and sentimental than probable.

Aston Cantlow church, where Shakespeare's grandfather, Robert Arden, is buried.

Two daughters, Joan and Margaret, had come before William. Margaret died in infancy before the birth of her brother, and Joan was certainly dead by 1569 when a second Joan Shakespeare was christened. To her, and to the siblings Gilbert born in 1566, Anne born in 1571 (and died in 1579), Richard born in 1574, and Edmund born in 1580, William was the eldest brother.

As an Alderman of Stratford, John Shakespeare was entitled to have his son educated free at the local Grammar School, and there is neither evidence nor doubt that Shakespeare learned his Latin there. In spite of Ben Jonson's notorious claim that he knew 'small *Latin*, and less *Greek*', he was clearly a sound Latinist with a particular affection in his younger days for Ovid. But his plays suggest a normal attitude of distaste for boyhood hours passed in silence, memorising and construing, and he evinces little respect for his fictional schoolmasters as a class. We may infer that schooldays were not the happiest of Shakespeare's life, and there is no reason to challenge the widespread feeling that the many enthusiastic references to country sports in the plays indicate ways in which young Will probably preferred to pass his time.

Entry in Stratford parish register recording Shakespeare's birth.

Since he was to become a successful actor, we may also reasonably surmise that he saw and enjoyed the visits of companies of players to Stratford during his boyhood. In 1569, while John Shakespeare was Bailiff of Stratford, the Queen's Players came to town and performed in the Guild Hall before him and his fellow citizens. The Bailiff paid them 9s. (nine shillings) for their performance, and showed himself to be a not uncritical spectator by prescribing a mere 12d. (twelve pence) for the next company to play at Stratford.

Will was five at the time, and we cannot tell whether he was kept at home out of his father's way, or allowed to see the players. But since Stratford was again visited by touring actors in Will's tenth, twelfth, thirteenth, sixteenth, seventeenth and eighteenth years we may take it as virtually certain that the young man was acquainted with theatre before his marriage, and acquainted with it as a rare and exciting occasion.

The Queen's Players were also known as her Interluders, a reference to the old fashioned type of play still in vogue in the 1560s and 70s. Like the older morality plays, Tudor interludes showed characters who were personifications of such abstract qualities as Wit, Reason, and Virtuous Life, on the one hand, and Idleness, Insolence, and Adultery, on the other. The virtues had elevated, poetical speeches, and presented a stately pageant. The vices enjoyed racier language with quick to-and-fro cross-talk in their dialogue, and a good deal of slapstick. Occasionally imaginative interludes gave the vices simulated plebeian names instead of mere abstractions – Tom Tosspot and Rafe Roister, for example. Sometimes the triumph of a noble figure from classical history or literature might be interspersed with the low comedy. But the mode of the serious scenes remained rhetorical, stately and essentially inactive. The young Shakespeare watched theatre which was comparatively primitive – astonishingly so when compared with the psychological density, emotional range and mimetic realism of his own plays.

One of the frescoes in the Guild Chapel at Stratford which was painted over during John Shakespeare's term as Chamberlain. Relics of the Catholic religion, after Queen Mary's death, were erased. This drawing of the fresco, restored by Thomas Fisher, was published in 1808.

Will Shakespeare was thirteen when his father purchased the western section of the 'Birthplace' block in Henley Street, and this expansion of his home marked the high-water mark of the glover's fortunes. He made application for a coat-of-arms, a social promotion, in effect, to his wife's family's class. And then he silently allowed the process to remain incomplete. Alderman Shakespeare started to miss council meetings. In the past he had been one of the most loyal attenders, present at a meeting of the brave rump of the council who sat in an orchard to avoid contagion during the great plague in the year of Will's birth. Now he avoided all meetings, though he had not quarrelled with his fellow councillors, who were at pains to relieve him of the taxes he owed for the maintenance of soldiers and his contribution to the poor rates.

This financial help was apparently not enough. John Shakespeare stopped buying property, and started to sell off his wife's inheritance. He sold her reversionary interest in property at Snitterfield. He let Asbies at a nominal rent, and probably took much-needed cash in compensation. He mortgaged land in Wilmcote to Mary's brother-in-law, Edmund Lambert, and lost it despite later bitter lawsuits. In 1587 his fellow-councillors gave up hope that he would ever recover sufficiently to return to their number, and they appointed a new alderman in his place, 'for that Mr Shakespeare doth not come to the halls when they be warned nor hath not done of long time'.

In 1592 he was noted as an absentee from church, and his retirement from public life is explained in the note that he and some others 'come not to church for fear of process for debt'. So from the time he was fifteen, William Shakespeare was in a home of falling fortune, and knew the strain of financial anxieties around him. He had been born—not with a silver spoon—but at least with good pewter in his mouth. Now it was turning to tin, and the effect on him seems to have been that he kept a touchy concern that his social status be not undervalued, and a decidedly bourgeois awareness of the need to establish his own financial security.

John Shakespeare's absence from church has been claimed as evidence that he—and more extravagantly, his son William—must have been Roman Catholic. But there is no reason to doubt the note explaining John Shakespeare's recusancy, especially when it is taken in conjunction with the hurried sale of his wife's property.

Nor need any weight be laid on the discovery and subsequent loss of a Catholic 'Spiritual Testament' (a declaration of faith, on a model devised by Cardinal Borromeo) which purported to be John Shakespeare's and to have been found in the roof of the Henley Street house during retiling in the eighteenth century. Eighteenth-century Stratford was the source of a good many spurious Shakespeare relics, and the fact that the

Shakespeare's birthplace, Stratford: the room where he is supposed to have been born.

document apparently described John as a butcher, rather than a glover or 'whittawer' (curer of fine skins for glovemaking) suggests that its author was more acquainted with late seventeenth-century tradition than sixteenth-century facts. That the document was written in a fair hand points away from John too. No signature of his survives, and he usually marked documents requiring his verification with an ideogram representing a pair of glover's dividers.

After Queen Mary's reign, the Stratford local worthies, like authorities elsewhere in the country, were much concerned with establishing a Protestant Church of England, and sweeping away the relics of Marian Catholicism. Adrian Quiney, a close friend of the Shakespeares, was prominent in this work, and has been described as the leader of the Protestant majority on the Stratford council. John Shakespeare, as Stratford Chamberlain, seems to have had no objection to replacing the altar in the Guild Chapel with a communion table, and painting out its charming but Papist frescoes.

What was John Shakespeare like personally? One most attractive report comes down to us: 'a merry apple-Cheeked old man—that said—Will was a good honest Fellow, but he durst have cracked a jest with him at any time'. Alas, this report cites as its authority a man born after John Shakespeare's death, so that it must be regarded as suspect. It is satisfactory that the reporter rightly knew John to be a glover, but suspiciously indicative of approaching Restoration attitudes that wit should be seen as the hallmark of a poet. Shakespeare's own contemporaries would not have felt that 'cracking a jest' was his greatest feat. We must sadly conclude that we do not know whether John Shakespeare was merry and apple-cheeked or not. We can only be certain that he was a successful and apparently honest local dignitary who fell upon hard times in his early middle age.

Anne Hathaway

SOMEWHERE, sometime, during the late summer of 1582, seventeen-year-old Will Shakespeare was making love to Anne Hathaway, seven or eight years his elder. She was probably the daughter of Richard Hathaway of Shottery, and lived at Hewland's Farm, the picturesque, half-timbered building now known as Anne Hathaway's Cottage. Richard Hathaway died in July 1582, close to the time that Anne conceived her first child, and he left her the sum of ten marks (£6.13s.4d.) to be paid on the day of her marriage.

On 27 November 1582, a special license was issued from Worcester for William Shakespeare to be married at his parish church without the usual triple calling of the banns. The following day, the usual bond indemnifying the Bishop against any impropriety in the issue of the license was posted by two Shottery men who had been friends of Richard Hathaway.

Special license was necessary for a wedding at this time of year, as three weeks delay would have brought the young couple into Advent, a prohibited season during which marriage could not take place. A subsequent

Hewlands Farm, Shottery, the home of Anne Hathaway before her marriage.

The classroom in Stratford Grammar School where Shakespeare is believed to have studied.

failure to marry in January would have brought them to another prohibited season, and the marriage would have been postponed till April. Which would have been embarrassing, as the child Anne was carrying was to be born in May.

There is one distinct problem about the documentation of Shakespeare's marriage. The license issued in the Worcester Diocese was recorded as permitting him to marry one Anne Whately of Temple Grafton. Whoever she might be (if she ever existed) she is never heard of again. From the bond posted the very next day until the day of her death in 1623, Mistress Shakespeare was consistently identified as the former Anne Hathaway. It is most likely that the clerk completing the register made a slip of the pen. He had recorded the name 'Whately' at a slightly earlier point in the register, and the names 'Whately' and 'Hathwey' (the spelling in the bond) contain enough common letters to distract a busy man.

The reference to Temple Grafton instead of Shottery is another small puzzle. It has been suggested that Anne's mother might have come from Temple Grafton, and she might have been living with kinsfolk there since her father's death.

Deeply embarrassed by the notion of a shotgun wedding for their national institution, Victorian scholars earnestly postulated a 'pre-marriage contract' or formal betrothal, which, they argued, would justify a devout young man in apparently anticipating his marriage – itself a ceremony which merely formalized the dowry.

But the facts and dates are clear enough. Shakespeare married as a minor. His wife was several years older than he. Their first child was born six months after the wedding.

Susanna Shakespeare was baptized on 26 May 1583. Not a popular Elizabethan christian name, its Old Testament origin hints at a Puritan bias, and Richard Hathaway's will suggests that he may have had Puritan leanings. The young Shakespeares' two other children, twins born two years later, were given names of more certainly identifiable provenance. Hamnet and Judith Sadler were a couple who lived in High Street Stratford. Hamnet remained a lifelong friend of Shakespeare's, witnessing and remembered in his will. These two were probably godparents to the twins, who were named after them.

Little more is known about Anne Hathaway Shakespeare. She stayed in Stratford for the rest of her life, living in Henley Street as long as her husband was domiciled there on his visits to the town, and moving to New Place when he bought the great house. In 1601, Thomas Whittington, an old Shottery shepherd who had worked for the Hathaways, left 40s. for the poor of the parish in his will, noting that it was 'in the hand of Anne Shakespeare, wife unto Mr William Shakespeare'. And in Shakespeare's own will, notoriously, Anne was left 'my

Grant of arms to John Shakespeare, 1596.

second best bed with the furniture'. Anne herself died in 1623, and was buried near her husband inside Holy Trinity church, Stratford.

What are we to say, then, about the fairly familiar feeling, by now achieving legendary status, that Shakespeare's marriage was not happy? The most important fact in support of the feeling is that Shakespeare passed most of his working life away from his wife, returning to Stratford only when the theatres were closed, and living in lodgings in London. The inference that this indicates an unhappy marriage is supported by the fact that the majority of his fellow-actors lived with their wives in respectable bourgeois city households into which they took apprentices. Those not living with wives were all bachelors: Shakespeare was the only member of his particular company to live apart from his wife during the working year.

If the name Susanna and the will of Richard Hathaway really do indicate a Puritan tendency in the Hathaways, including Anne, then she would not have been at all happy about her husband's chosen profession. To the Puritans, theatres were quite simply the works of the devil. But making Anne a Puritan is moving steadily into speculative realms.

On the other hand, we must notice that Shakespeare never severed his ties with Stratford. While his public career as an actor and his lasting reputation as a writer were made in London, his private security rested in the steady acquisition of property in Stratford where he bought houses, land and tithes; he kept up contact with Stratford friends like the Quineys while he was in London; he retired to Stratford; and he died and was buried there. In his will he made eight small bequests to Stratford men outside his family. Only three of his London cronies were similarly remembered.

And if Stratford was thus central to his sense of self, he can hardly be seen as deserting the wife and children who would always be waiting at home for him. We may suspect, from his failure to take Anne to London with him, that the marriage was not a deeply emotional tie; but we must conclude, from the way he chose to end his life, that the marriage could not be said to have broken down irreparably.

Even the matter of the second-best bed is one of question and debate. Anne *might* have been auto-matically entitled to 'widow's thirds'—a one-third portion of her husband's estate ensuring her inde-pendence till her death, and not requiring an entry in the will. But widow's thirds were a locally determined matter, and it is not clear that Stratford awarded them. So that she *might* have been given a bed and bedclothes, and been left to trust to her daughters' kindness to find a roof to put it under! And why the *second*-best bed? This looks like a gratuitous insult, surely? Yet at least one other will of the period, which is undisguisedly warm in its memory of the testator's wife, leaves her a similar bequest. We just don't know what this—the most famous bequest in English history—really signified.

The Lost Years

IN 1592 SHAKESPEARE was in London, recognised as an actor, and enjoying an increasing reputation as a writer of plays. Clearly he must have been there for some years previously. But exactly when he went to London, why he left Stratford, and what, if anything, he did before becoming an actor, are questions to which no certain answer can be given. The bald facts are that Shakespeare must have been in Stratford in 1584 when Hamnet and Judith were conceived, and we do not know where and what he was over the next seven years.

The lost years have given rise to some of the best-known legends in Shakespeareana. The traditional collocation of stories is familiar: young Shakespeare was always a little wild in Stratford, and famous for his drinking. He was arrested for poaching deer in Charlcote Park, and brought before its magisterial owner, Sir Thomas Lucy. Feeling himself hard done by when the outraged landlord ordered him a whipping, Shakespeare composed some abusive doggerel verse on Lucy, which redoubled the prosecution and led to the poacher-poet's flight from Stratford. In London he set up as a horse-holder at the theatre doors, becoming so successful in guarding patrons' mounts while they enjoyed the play that he soon had to employ boys to help him. He left to find employment inside the theatre, first as the prompter's assistant, or call-boy, and at last as an actor and writer.

None of this familiar history can be certified as true. But some parts are more likely than others. The deer-poaching story was current in Stratford about fifty years after Shakespeare's death, where four separate investigators heard versions of it. By the early eighteenth century, 'a very aged gentleman living in the neighbourhood of Stratford' or one Thomas Jones, aged ninety, of Tardebigge, had been prevailed upon to recall the first verse of the offending ballad. It apparently ran thus (with its rustic pronunciation lovingly preserved by the transcribers):

A parliament member, a justice of peace,
At home a poor scarecrow, at London an ass,
If lousy is Lucy, as some volk miscall it,
Then Lucy is lousy whatever befall it.
    He thinks himself great
    Yet an ass in his state
We allow by his ears but with asses to mate.
    If Lucy is lousy, as some volk miscall it,
    Sing lousy Lucy, whatever befall it.

Title-page of a Tudor Interlude, showing the allegorized abstractions as characters.

London printed by *George Purslowe*, and are to be sold by at Christ

Charlecote Hall, home of Sir Thomas Lucy, the magistrate traditionally believed to have arrested Shakespeare for poaching.

Suspiciously enough, the apparently meandering rhythm fits *Lillaburlero*, a popular tune for scurrilous balladry in the late seventeenth century but, of course, not yet composed in Shakespeare's day.

But four independent sources tracing the story force us to be cautious about rejecting it out of hand. This particular legend may well contain a grain of truth. Sir Thomas Lucy was a considerable magnate. He owned Sutton Park, Hampton Lucy and Sherborne in addition to Charlcote. He was knighted during Elizabeth's progress through Warwickshire in 1565. He was High Sheriff of his county, and MP for Warwickshire. His coat of arms bore 'three luces hauriant argent' – three vertical silver pike, punning, of course, as heraldry so often does, upon his name. Those who think Shakespeare likely to bear a grudge for twelve years, and then take a rather remote and tangential revenge, maintain that the description of Justice Shallow's arms – 'the dozen white louses' – in *The Merry Wives of Windsor* points derisively at Lucy.

The Lucy family might well become targets of local stories of poaching. In the 1580s Sir Thomas tried to have an Act passed to make poaching a felony. And in 1610 his grandson, a third Sir Thomas, brought a case in the Star Chamber against a poacher who had robbed his deer park. Clearly they were unamiable game-hoarding squires. But in the all-important 'lost years', 1585-1592, the Lucys did not have a deer park as such; only a 'free-warren'. They might have run roe-deer (though not fallow-deer) in such a warren, and one variant does indicate that Shakespeare was after rabbits as well as venison. The plays, however, suggest a clear interest in deer: there are important references in *Titus Andronicus*, *Henry VI pt 2*, *Love's Labour's Lost* and *As You Like It*.

The legend that young Shakespeare was a mighty toper, and the precise anecdote that he and his mates slept in a drunken stupor under a specified crabtree after losing a drinking match at Bidford arose at a time far too remote from his life for it to be given credence, even though the enthusiasm of eighteenth-century bardolaters for the story led to the tree's being entirely destroyed at the hands of relic-hunters.

Apart from possibly poaching and implausibly boozing, what is young Shakespeare supposed to have done with himself before becoming an actor? Only one tradition here has attracted serious modern favour. It derives from William Beeston, the son of an actor who worked with Shakespeare's company in 1598. Beeston's information about Shakespeare's personality is unsensational and unpredictable, and therefore seems likely to be reliable. He tells us that Shakespeare 'was not a company keeper, lived in Shoreditch, wouldn't be

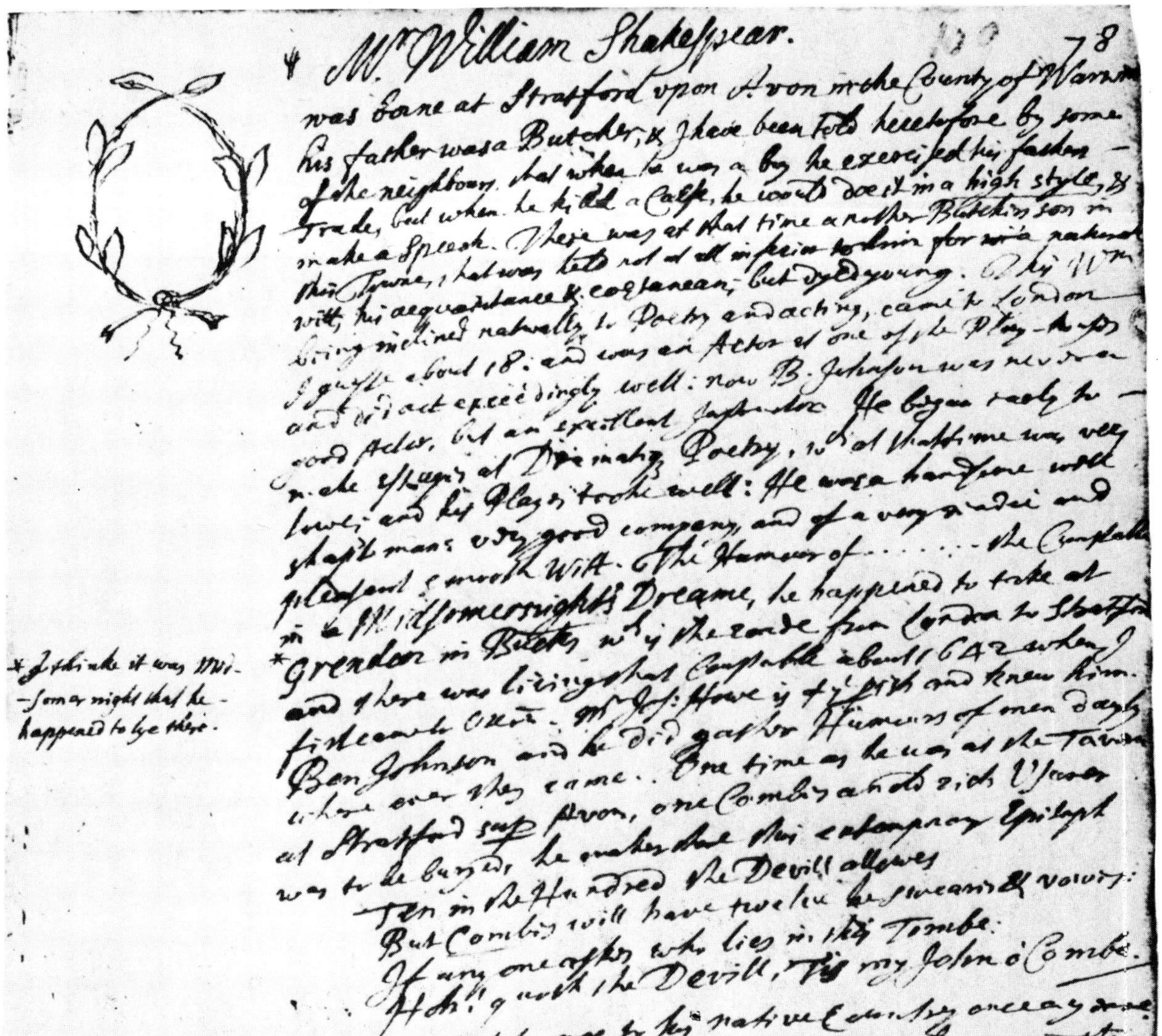

Mr William Shakespear.

[Manuscript notes by John Aubrey, in a difficult 17th-century hand. Marginal notes at left include:]

* I thinke it was Mid-
somer night that he
happened to lye there.

v. his Epitaph
in Dugdales Warw.

B. Johnsons Vnder-
-wood.

from Mr ... Beeston.

[Caption below the manuscript:]

Antiquarian John Aubrey's notes on Shakespeare,
compiled around 1680. The second line plunges into
demonstrable error: 'his father was a Butcher'. But the
final marginal note, 'From Mr Beeston' directs us to a
source which makes scholars take at least a part of this
traditional matter seriously.

17

In spite of many quarterings as the Lucy family married with other armigerous families, the three luces still held pride of place in the top left hand corner of their coat-of-arms.

masters (which does not seem like wry self-satire). Other theories have been proposed, usually on the strength of supposed specialist knowledge revealed in the plays. Thus we are told Shakespeare 'must have been' a lawyer, or a soldier, or a seaman, or a scrivener. With the exception of the last theory, all have been propounded by people who, happily, chanced to belong to the very profession they found themselves sharing with their hero. None of them carries the slightest conviction.

The tradition of the horse-holding is first mentioned in 1748, but is then derived from Sir William Davenant, the cavalier poet and theatre manager who had known Shakespeare when he stayed in his father's Oxford inn on his way to Stratford and claimed to be Shakespeare's godson. But Davenant had himself been dead for sixty years when this story was fathered on him, and John Aubrey, the Restoration antiquary who made notes of gossip collected about Davenant and Shakespeare, some emanating from Davenant, made no mention of it.

One phrase in the familiar old tradition may hint at a tiny grain of truth: 'Shakespeare, when he first came from the country to the playhouse, was not admitted to act.' This seems likely enough. Elizabethan actors were skilled professionals, and would hardly have taken on a stage-struck youngster, too old to play girls' parts, on the strength of some supposed talent. It has even been suggested that Shakespeare's company only accepted members who had completed a formal apprenticeship, and that Shakespeare's lost years must have been taken up with his own training. This is possible, though it tends too much to equate the rather informal system by which actors took apprentices with the rigid statutory apprenticeships of the crafts and guilds.

At any rate, at some time during the lost years, while England trembled in anticipation of, and rejoiced at the defeat of the Great Armada, William Shakespeare committed himself to the theatre. He may well have left Stratford simply by joining one of the companies that visited it in those years. The Earl of Leicester's Men, for example, were there in 1587, and in the same year, the Queen's Men (not the same company as the old interluders Shakespeare might have watched in his childhood) were in a position to welcome a recruit when they reached Stratford, one of their number, William Knell, having been stabbed in the throat and killed at Thame.

But with Shakespeare's career as an actor poised for launching, it is time to consider the state of the theatre in the last twenty years of Elizabeth's reign.

debauched, & if invited to wrote; he was in pain' – (that is, he cried off wild parties with the excuse of sickness). Beeston was right about Shoreditch, and so there is today great willingness to accept his statement that Shakespeare 'understood Latin pretty well: for he had been in his younger days a Schoolmaster in the Country'.

Modern scholars observe that Shakespeare would have been an 'abecedarius' or humble teaching assistant, not having the qualification to be a school's master. 'In the Country' might, of course, be London-bred Beeston's view of Stratford, and being 'a Schoolmaster' might in the actor's eyes cover any sort of pupil-teaching. To push harder than this for Shakespeare the young pedagogue is to ignore his plays' rather obvious mockery of school-

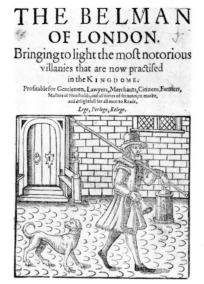

THE BELMAN
OF LONDON.
Bringing to light the most notorious
villanies that are now practised
in the K I N G D O M E.
Profitable for Gentlemen, Lawyers, Merchants, Citizens, Farmers,
Masters of Housholds, and all sortes of servants, to marke,
and delightfull for all men to Reade.
Lege, Perlege, Relege.

The Theatre

BY 1590 THE ENGLISH theatre had been transformed. Interludes were a thing of the past. Tragedies (often historical) and comedies dominated the stage, and a new generation of educated men had come to London to write material for the actors.

The developments had been prefigured earlier in the century. During the 1530s, John Bale had found a way of using tragic drama to support Henry VIII's quarrel with the Pope. Bale's *King John* ingeniously combined historical characters (John, Stephen Langton, the Pope) with traditional allegorical morality figures (Sedition, Treason, Verity) and symbolic figures representing classes, masses and special interests (Widow England, Clergy, Commonalty, Nobility). The play as a whole put forward a Protestant propagandist's interpretation of John as a heroic opponent of Papal supremacy, poisoned and traduced by unpatriotic Papist monks.

The theme of the play is still to be found in Shakespeare's *King John*: the mixed form was reinforced by later plays, notably Thomas Preston's *Cambyses, King of Persia* (c. 1569) in which an Interlude-style Vice called Ambidexter tempts the completely realistic judge Sisamnes and his king, Cambyses; representative individual lower class rogues called Ruf, Huf and Snuf appear, as well as class-symbolic figures (Commons' Cry, Commons' Complaint); allegorical figures are present (Diligence, Cruelty, Shame); and Venus and Cupid enter to influence the amatory fortunes of the main characters.

Pure tragedy was launched in 1561 by Thomas Sackville with some assistance from Thomas Norton. Their *Gorboduc* was as perfectly classical a work as could then be devised. The play was divided into five acts. Allegorical characters were abandoned; after the classical manner, all violent action took place off stage and was reported. Equally after the classical manner there was a great deal of such violence. In the course of

the play one son murders the other, and is then murdered by his mother, who is promptly killed with her husband.

The model for this family bloodbath was Seneca, the Roman philosopher-playwright, whose gory rhetoric had not been intended for the theatrical presentation, but who was mistaken by the Tudors for the ancient world's great master of theatre. The plot was drawn from ancient British legendary history, and in this and some other respects bears a primitive resemblance to *King Lear*. The play was given an amateur performance by the students of the Inner Temple, and won the admiration of Sir Philip Sidney. Its slow progression of long speeches in blank verse of leaden accuracy could never have won popular favour, but its *succès d'éstime* made it influential. When Preston's *Cambyses* substituted bombastic four-teeners for frigid blank verse, brought the physical horrors spectacularly onto the stage, and retained some allegorical characters, he showed ways in which Senecan tragedy might be modified to meet the sensational and conservative taste of popular audiences.

Comedy developed from a pedantic wish to tame the Interludes and moralities, and bring them into classical form. Nicolas Udall, headmaster of Eton, wrote *Ralph Roister Doister* around 1540. He retained a vice-like agent of mischief named Matthew Merrygreeke, and gave other characters (like Ralph) names which immediately identified their simple characterisation. The claim that Udall wrote 'the first English comedy' rests on his following aspects of Latin comedy in his structure and characterisation. He followed the five-act division, and devised a plot which was a story to be enjoyed in its own right, rather than a thin basis for rhetorical moralising. And his plot was clearly influenced by Plautus, concerning the attempt of a braggart roisterer to woo a rich widow in the absence of her true affianced lover. Some of the characters derived from Plautus also. Roister

Tamburlaine

the Great.

Who, from a Scythian Shepheard,

by his rare and wonderfull Conquestes, be=
came a most puissant and mightie
Mornarch:

And (for his tyrannie, and terrour in warre)
was tearmed,

The Scourge of God.

The first part of the two Tragicall dif=
courses, as they were sundrie times most
stately shewed vpon Stages in the
Citie of London.

By the right honorable the Lord Admirall,
his seruauntes.

Now newly published.

Printed by Richard Iones, dwelling at the signe of
the Rose and Crowne ne ere Holborne
Bridge. 1590.

The title page of Marlowe's Tamburlaine. *Notice that
the performance of the play by the Admiral's Men is the
stressed selling point. Marlowe's authorship is mentioned
nowhere.*

Doister was a version of the Latin 'miles gloriosus' or braggart soldier–a favourite stock type for the later Elizabethans. Even Matthew Merrygreeke owed as much to the example of the Latin parasite as he did to the interlude vice.

One important aspect of *Ralph Roister Doister* is English and not classical. The names of the maidservants –Margaret Mumblecrust, Tibet Talkapace and Annot Alyface–show Udall alive to the traditionally comical aspects of ordinary life around him, and their conversation as they sit and spin is homely and English.

Solid, down-to-earth humour of daily life was developed further during the following decade in *Gammer Gurton's Needle*, where rustic neighbours, the magistrate and the vicar all fall out over the missing needle which is finally found, not stolen, but painfully lodged in Hodge's bottom. No classical model was needed for this: it had been present in English drama since the first miracle plays. And it remained, only growing a little more sophisticated, as the great period of Elizabethan and Jacobean drama emerged.

The 1560s saw two more elements introduced that were to influence the greater period of comedy. George Gascoigne's *Supposes* was a prose translation of Ariosto's *I Suppositi*. It introduced to English theatre one fashion of Italian comedy: a complicated love-tangle among courtly young people. It also offered one of the great agents of farcical comedy: disguise or impersonation leading to mistaken identities on stage, while the audience can perceive both the truth and the error, and enjoy the cross-purposes at which the characters find themselves. Meanwhile Richard Edwards' *Damon and Pythias* had introduced 'tragical comedy', a deliberate interweaving of genres, in which problems more moving than stylish were resolved, leaving a sense of disaster averted rather than mere charm.

The early 1570s saw the beginnings of the theatrical organisation which, by Shakespeare's day, was to make London the theatre capital of Europe. In 1572 the government passed an *Act for the punishment of Vagabonds*, which laid down that jugglers, tinkers, chapmen, pedlars, fencers, bearwards and common players were to be adjudged 'sturdy beggars' (able-bodied unemployed, who were to be whipped back to their parish of permanent residence) unless they were licensed by two justices of the peace, or were the accredited employees of a peer of the realm. There was at once a rush of players seeking acknowledgement and liveries from the nobility!

The small companies of players were expected to earn their own living by public performances in the yards of inns. Not even Tudor magnates were so prodigally cultured as to anticipate the need for an entire company of actors to perform solely for them. But a grandee magnificent enough to entertain the Queen might find it useful to have first call on the time of some players to amuse her majesty. And it was now essential for every professional actor to enlist himself under the patronage of such a lord. James Burbage made it clear that it was the uniform of service that mattered, not the pay, when he sued to the powerful Earl of Leicester on behalf of his fellows:

> vouchsafe to retain us at this present as your
> household servants and daily waiters, not that
> we mean to crave any further stipend or
> benefits at your Lordship's hands but our
> liveries as we have had, and also your
> honour's License to certify that we are your
> household Servants when we shall have
> occasion to travel amongst our friends as we
> do usually once a year.

The yearly travels were the summer provincial tours that took players to places like Stratford. There were also sporadic tours outside the City at times of plague, when the authorities firmly prohibited playing, as much to forfend the wrath of God against such sinful pleasures as to avoid contagion.

The court liked plays as part of its entertainment, and since Henry VIII's day, a Master of the Revels had been responsible for arranging the jollifications that enlivened every Christmas season. This court official was of the first importance to the players. Edmund Tilney, Master of the Revels from 1579 until 1607 was, indeed, a man of high consequence to English literature, for he was the civil servant responsible for selecting and presenting Shakespeare's work to the most influential and fashionable audience in the land. During his long term of office, the Master's role expanded from that of general stage manager and producer of a series of annual entertain-

impede the royal preference from time to time. In a petty matter like the theatre it was easy for the London alderman to keep up continuous sniping and harassment, against which the Queen could only offer general protection, and to details of which she might yield. Thus when she granted Leicester's Men a royal license, she added the order that plays inflicted on Puritan townsmen must only be such as Tilney had seen and approved. Political and religious censorship was definitely to be exercised against the greatest period of English theatre.

Cities and boroughs could always impede the players by discovering that particular places were unfortunately

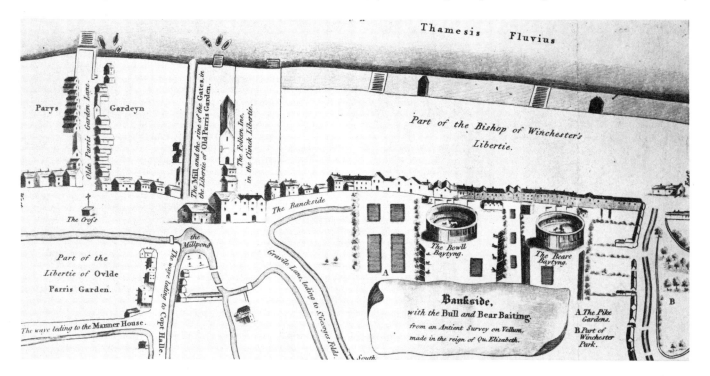

The Bankside, showing the Bishop of Winchester's Liberty. This was the location of a notable collection of brothels.

ments to overall controller of all professional and much amateur theatre, with responsibility for the censorship and licensing of plays, and the licensing of professional companies.

The Office of the Revels was situated at Clerkenwell, where Tilney had the use of the converted priory of St John. There were storerooms, a kitchen and garden, and most important, a great chamber where plays could be run through. Tilney selected the plays to be shown at court by watching specimen performances. As the players still had to earn their living by day, these often took place at night, and Tilney's lighting bill was heavy. He had charge of a store of costumes and properties, and was empowered to buy new materials each season. But the basic raw material remained the actors, who had to be protected from Puritan oppression if the shows were to go on.

The court was powerful, but not absolutely overwhelming in Elizabethan England. Local authorities, though technically deriving their power from the crown, could nonetheless appeal to local needs and conditions to

inappropriate for them. In 1574 the authorities of London drafted a general objection to acting in

> great Inns, having chambers and secret places adjoining to their open stages and galleries, inveigling and alluring of maids, specially orphans and good Citizens' Children under Age, to privy and unmeet Contracts.

In other words, Elizabethan innyard theatres were dangerously close to cheap private rooms and dark corridors where girls, excited by stage romance, might be tumbled and fumbled. The notion that such girls were peculiarly likely to be orphaned or under age may be dismissed as the usual overheated imagining of self-appointed censors. But the attack on theatre in the innyards had been mounted, and it behoved a forward-looking man of the theatre like James Burbage to take defensive measures.

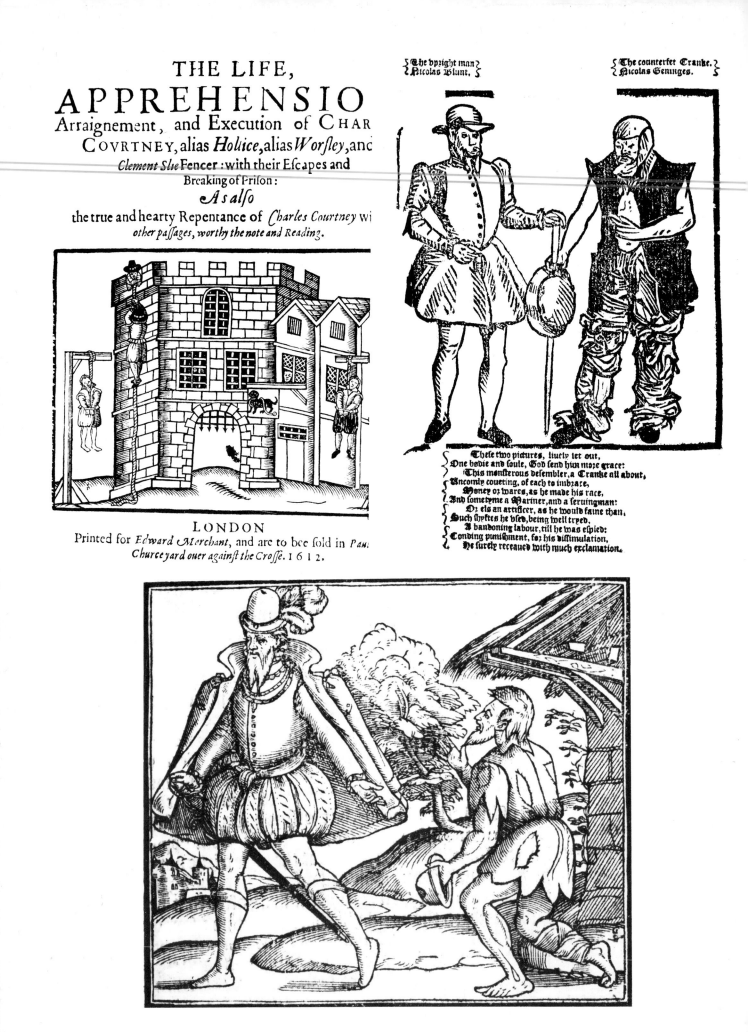

THE LIFE,
APPREHENSIO
Arraignement, and Execution of CHAR
COVRTNEY, alias *Hollice*, alias *Worſley*, and
Clement Slie Fencer : with their Eſcapes and
Breaking of Priſon :
As alſo
the true and hearty Repentance of *Charles Courtney* wi
other paſſages, worthy the note and Reading.

LONDON
Printed for *Edward Merchant*, and are to bee ſold in *Pau*
Churce yard ouer againſt the Croſſe. 1 6 1 2.

{The vpright man}
{Nicolas Blunt,}

{The counterfet Cranke.}
{Nicolas Geninges.}

Theſe two pictures, liuely ſet out,
One bodie and ſoule, God ſend him moe grace:
This monſterous deſembler, a Cranke all about,
Vncomly coueting, of each to imbrace,
Money or wares, as he made his race,
And ſometyme a Mariner, and a ſeruingman:
Or els an artificer, as he would faine than,
Such ſhyftes he vſed, being well tryed,
Abandoning labour, till he was eſpied:
Conding puniſhment, for his diſſimulation,
He ſurely receaued with much exclamation.

Burbage's action was swift, ingenious and historic. To escape the jurisdiction of the city authorities, yet retain the patronage of city audiences, he proposed acting just outside the boundaries of the City of London. To avoid interference with the business of acting by the business of innkeeping, he proposed performing on his own leased property. And to simplify production and the admission and seating of audiences, that property should be a custom-built house for staging plays. In 1576 James Burbage built the first English theatre.

Burbage was a joiner by training, and no doubt devised the structure of the wooden-frame playhouse. To provide capital for the venture (£650) he entered into partnership with his brother-in-law, John Brayne, a grocer who had already invested in theatrical ventures at the Red Lion Inn, Stepney. Land was leased from Giles Allen for fourteen years in the first instance, with the option of renewing for a further twenty-one years. In addition to rent, Allen was entitled to free seats in 'some one of the upper rooms'. A term of the lease which was to prove important entitled Burbage to remove any materials used in erecting buildings on the site.

The Theatre, as it was simply named, was in Shoreditch, about a mile north of the City boundaries, and it set the pattern for Elizabethan playhouses. There were three models that Burbage might have followed. Companies of boy actors from the London schools and choirs acted for the nobility in private, indoor houses (just as the players themselves performed in the great halls and chambers of their patrons on festive occasions). Although indoor entertainment offered advantageous protection against the weather, Burbage could not have built a large enough auditorium to cram in enough customers to make an indoor theatre a paying proposition.

The two other models available to Burbage were the innyard theatres, and the arenas employed for bull- or bear-baiting. He appears to have drawn on both of these, though we do not know in precise detail what either they or the Elizabethan theatre were like. But our general picture of Shakespeare's 'wooden O' is fair enough as far as it goes, though there are grey areas and important points in dispute.

The building was a circular or polygonal structure, about thirty feet high and fifty feet across. Three storeys of seating galleries projected into the circle from the outer walls, to a depth of twelve feet. This perimeter seating area was roofed with thatch in a great ring, leaving the central arena open to the sky. Thus far we have the equivalent of a bull-ring. But where the bull-

ring's arena would be cleared for the bulls and dogs, the Theatre filled the south-western half with a projecting stage, and permitted patrons (the groundlings) to stand in the other half of the arena, and at the edges of the stage, for the payment of one penny.

Over the stage itself, continuing the line of the thatch roof, was a large canopy, supported on heavy pillars that descended to and through the stage. The seating galleries were not continued unbroken behind the stage: a flat wall immediately behind the stage broke the smooth inner curve of the arena, and behind this lay what was colloquially called 'the tiring house', or actors' dressing room. Here costumes and properties were stored, and the actors awaited their cues to go onstage.

There were at least two doors leading on to the stage from the tiring house wall, and it is likely that some Elizabethan theatres also had a larger opening between the two which could be shuttered or curtained, from which spectacular chariots might have appeared in plays like Marlowe's *Tamburlaine*. It is no longer thought likely that such a curtained recess in the wall formed an 'inner stage' where scenes in pavilions or caves took place: it seems more likely that little booths might be built against the wall for such scenes, as mountebanks had long used booths at the back of platforms, and players had imitated them, and carried the practice (it is thought) into the innyards.

Halfway up the tiring house wall, a recess appeared, showing some more galleries. It is possible that these were the most expensive seats in the house, the private 'lords' rooms'. But it is equally possible that this space could be curtained over and used as an acting space for scenes 'above' (at windows, or on besieged city walls) which are familiar in Shakespeare. De Witt's famous and important sketch of the Swan Theatre seems to show spectators in this position: the sketch of the theatre on the title page of Richards' *Messalina*, on the other hand, seems to show scenic curtains at upper and lower levels of the tiring house wall. Certainly Sir Walter Raleigh expected to see 'drawn curtains when the play is done', and saw something very different from the image the words call to our minds. But he might have been thinking of curtains hanging from the front of the stage to the ground. The understage area was used with trapdoors, and from its bowels, little boys with firecrackers rushed out in plays which featured devils and imps.

At the top of the tiring house, all later theatres certainly, and so the Theatre presumably, carried one or more pitch-roofed gabled attic rooms, known as the 'huts', which may have housed musicians and sound effects men (rolling cannon balls to simulate thunder over the actors' heads). Beside or over these, a small balcony permitted a trumpeter to signal the start of a performance and run up the flag that signalled a play in performance.

portitus

sedilia

orchestia

ingressus

mimorum aedes.

tectum

proscænium.

planeties fiue arena.

Ex obferuationibus Londinenfibus Johannis de witt

*Johannes de Witt's famous sketch of the interior of Francis Langley's Swan Theatre, on Bankside. It shows very clearly the three storeys of galleries, the tiring-house behind the stage (*mimorum aedes, *or actors' house), the 'heavens' supported on two pillars to shelter the rear of the stage, and the 'hut' above with the theatre's standard and the trumpeter's balcony. Its two doors into the tiring-house do not look suitable for transformation into an inner stage. But it poses three problems. The gallery in the tiring-house wall seems to be occupied by spectators rather than actors 'above' or are they musicians? The arrangement supporting the stage is puzzling: are we shown two large baulks, or trestles? Or are they gaps in curtaining presumed to be hanging from the stage? And the entrance (*ingressus*) looks more like crude steps up to the gallery than a door in to the theatre.*

24

By 1577 performances at the Theatre had begun. And in the same year Henry Lanman erected the Curtain, a very small distance to the south of the Theatre in Shoreditch. The great period of Elizabethan theatrical history was now truly under way, with these two theatres offering their stages to the great companies now coming into being. In the winter, to save citizens the walk through dirty weather, the actors continued to use innyards, notably those of the Bell and the Cross Keys in Gracechurch Street. In times of plague, the companies would 'break' and re-form as actors grouped in new combinations for the enforced provincial or foreign tours.

In 1583 Elizabeth directed Tilney to select 'a company of players for her majesty', and for five years the Queen's Men held unrivalled domination over the other companies. Richard Tarlton, their leading player, was already in the Queen's service as one of her private jesters. He was the most famous comedian of the late sixteenth century, and devised or perfected many tricks that other clowns carried on into the stage tradition. Audiences loved his habit of poking his cross-eyed, curly-

The title-page of Marlowe's Dr Faustus *shows that the Admiral's Men adopted their patron's new title when he was elevated to the earldom of Nottingham.*

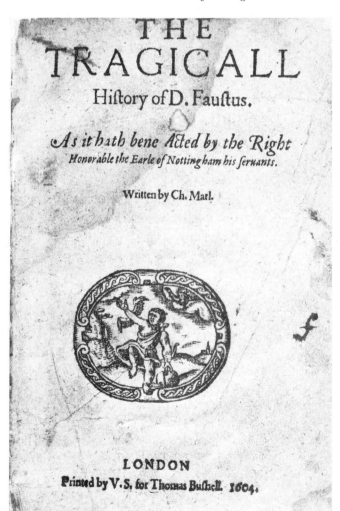

Forty years after its original production, Kyd's The Spanish Tragedy *was still being corrected, amended, enlarged and published. The scene shows Hieronimo discovering his son Horatio hanged in a bower, while the assassins (only one of whom is visible) try to silence Horatio's lover, Bel-Imperia.*

topped head round a curtain and pulling faces at them before the play began. He wore a russet suit, with buttoned cap and strapped boots, and played the tabor (a tiny drum that could be beaten with one hand while the other stopped a little pipe). For a generation he was remembered as the acme of stage comedy.

By the time the Queen's Men were brought together, there was already a third theatre in the vicinity of London. The Surrey village of Newington, about a mile south of London Bridge, was the site of the butts where citizens were encouraged to practise their archery. And at Newington Butts someone—possibly Philip Henslowe, the Southwark moneylender—opened a small theatre about which we know very little. The change of direction outside London was interesting, forecasting the theatrical importance of the South Bank.

By 1585 Henslowe certainly did own the Newington Butts theatre, and in that year he leased a piece of land nearer the City, in the Liberties of the Clink on Bankside.

Here he built a new theatre, the Rose (named like the Curtain after the land on which it stood), and his subsequent career was noteworthy. He became the principal Elizabethan theatre manager, rivalling the Burbages, and his stepdaughter married the most famous and successful tragic actor of the day.

The site of the Rose was well chosen. Londoners had only to be ferried across the Thames to it, and they were then in a district whose freedom from the jurisdiction of the city fathers had already brought it such notable entertainment institutions as the Bear Garden, and the considerable collection of brothels whose ground landlord was, notoriously, the Bishop of Winchester.

New, exciting writers were required for so vital a force as the theatre had now become, and the demand was satisfied by a group of young men whose education and brilliance gave them the nickname 'the University Wits'. They transformed the drama, and developed in the 1580s the flexible instrument of blank verse, grand rhetoric, low comedy, scintillating banter and delicate romance that Shakespeare was to inherit and raise to even greater heights. The Oxford men among the Wits were John Lyly, George Peele and Thomas Lodge. Lyly, the eldest and most important of them, had gained fame with his prose romance *Euphues*, which set a fashion in refined, balanced rhetoric, more stylish than meaningful. He wrote for the companies of boy actors until their suppression in 1590, and gave them witty, modish comedies, with one eye on classical poise and another on modern Italian fashion.

The Cambridge men were altogether greater. While Lyly must have had some influence on *Love's Labour's Lost*, Nashe, the Cambridge satirist, was probably himself lightly satirised in it. And Robert Greene and Christopher Marlowe were the only two writers whose work might have led a prophet to predict that literature of the stature of Shakespeare's might emerge from the late Elizabethan stage.

Marlowe was the most important writer of pre-Shakespearean drama. Young, freethinking, ambitious, homosexual, occasionally employed by Francis Walsingham's government secret service, Marlowe astounded London theatregoers with the grandeur of vision, theatrical spectacle and resonant versification of his *Tamburlaine the Great*. Gorgeous costumes, skilful fencing and nimble dancing were all familiar to theatregoers as part of the show. But Marlow offered a captive king used as a footstool, and beating out his brains against the bars of the wheeled cage from which he bewailed his overthrow; he envisaged a conqueror yoking kings to his chariot and lashing them across the stage. Marlowe's atheistic mind was excited by the amoral truths of *realpolitik*, and good Elizabethan Englishmen, already shocked by Niccolo Machiavelli's dreadful suggestion that political success had nothing to do with virtue, were

The Earl of Leicester, patron of Will Kemp, Thomas Pope and George Bryan.

Ferdinando, Lord Strange, later the Earl of Derby, was the patron of Shakespeare's fellows Kemp, Pope, Hemmings, Phillips and Bryan after the death of Leicester in 1588, and before they came under the patronage of Lord Hunsdon, the Lord Chamberlain.

thrilled and horrified to discover a writer who exhibited Machiavellian politics on the stage before them.

Tamburlaine was a suitable role for Edward Alleyn, the great tragedian. Alleyn was originally a member of the Earl of Worcester's Men, the only company to offer serious competition to the Queen's Men during the 1580s. His preferred roles were dominating, ranting ones. Marlowe's 'mighty line', in which three weighty stresses relieved blank verse of its iambic singsong, gave him speeches much to his taste. Tamburlaine's famous abuse of the kings drawing his chariot exemplifies the effect (Asia being trisyllabic):

Hólla, ye pamper'd jádes of Asiá!

Whát, can ye draw but twénty miles a dáy?

Marlowe had hopes of rising in the public service, and did not feel entirely dependent on writing to make a living. His friend and imitator Robert Greene had no friends at court, and was willy-nilly a full time hack writer. He eagerly copied Marlowe's successes, writing in *Orlando*

Furioso a ranting tragedy which gave Alleyn another Tamburlaine-like role, and copying Marlowe's *Doctor Faustus* by exhibiting spectacular conjuring and wizardry in his *Friar Bacon and Friar Bungay*. Literary history is kind to innovators, and Greene's apparent lack of originality has led to his being dismissed to the background. Yet he was, in fact, one of the most charming and versatile writers of his day, and his work seems to have influenced Shakespeare as much as any of his predecessors'.

What Greene injected into the drama was a delicate and tactful way of writing about love. In Greene's successful comedies (*James IV* and *Friar Bacon and Friar Bungay*) a sub-plot of love interest is managed without either the frigid rhetoric of (say) Tamburlaine and his Zenocrate, or the sugary and superficial ornamentation loved by Lyly and his followers. Greene is able to write about lovers who sound like lovers, and to deal with popular romance's favourite theme – class disparity

Richard Tarlton, the most famous clown of pre-Shakespearean Elizabethan theatre.

between lovers – without popular romance's frivolous woodenness. He suggests domestic sincerity by having his noble and royal lovers call their queens and ladies by shortened names – Peggy, or Doll.

This capacity to suggest realistic and unaffected love is, perhaps, surprising inasmuch as Greene was a notorious debauchee. After travelling on the continent, he had returned to live among whores, petty criminals and boozers on the underside of London life. He was the first English Bohemian writer, and exploited his knowledge of the underworld in a series of pamphlets describing methods of crime and petty fraud. Everything about his life suggests wasted talents. Yet his writing constantly surprises by its unaffectedness and delicacy. Greene abandoned the wife who reproved him for his dissolute ways, fathered a bastard on a whore, and ebulliently named him Fortunatus. Yet he also wrote the simple and beautiful lullaby 'Weep not my wanton' which touchingly but unsentimentally notes the pain of separation from each other and their child endured by unmarried parents. An interesting man, Greene, and his path crossed Shakespeare's not too long after the latter's arrival in London.

One other writer made a major contribution to the drama Shakespeare found. Thomas Kyd was the son of a London scrivener, and appears to have been trained for the law. He was a friend of Marlowe, and enjoyed almost as great a theatrical success with his melodrama *The Spanish Tragedy*, and a lost early version of *Hamlet*.

Kyd was not a great writer. The sub-title of *The Spanish Tragedy* indicates rather well his incapacity to restrain sensationalism from toppling into bathos: *Hieronimo's Mad Again!* does not suggest very deathless drama. But Kyd did know how to pile gripping sensations together in a strongly worked plot. Ghosts, murders, distraught lovers, discovered bodies, brooding revengers, madness, assassination, silence under torture, self-mutilation: all this Grand Guignol stuff is relentlessly packed into three hours by Kyd. The horrors of *The Spanish Tragedy* come so thick and fast that they would be unbearably harrowing if one could take them seriously today.

But so sensational a play succeeded well with a popular audience. It held the stage for at least fifteen years, enjoying occasional updating and revision; and long after Shakespeare and Ben Jonson had carried the drama to heights Kyd could never have scaled, conservative playgoers still seem to have complained that they didn't write plays like *The Spanish Tragedy* any more!

Kyd's lasting importance lies in the seal he set on tragedy of revenge as a form. The Bible stated clearly that Vengeance was the Lord's: He would repay. Yet the new continental code of honour spreading from Italy indicated that no true gentleman could brook an affront – let alone a serious injury – without exacting the fullest revenge. Was this murderous Italian amorality, like Machiavellism? Or did this mean that the truly noble were tragically condemned to flout the will of God and suffer damnation for actions with which any man of proper pride must sympathise? Kyd and the later dramatists were able to wring tragic resolution from the sufferer who achieves his desired revenge, and immediately dies himself: in the end the form accreted conventions which made its problems easily available to all theatregoers. The crown, though not the conclusion of revenge tragedy is *Hamlet*.

The end of the 1580s saw the end of the unchallenged domination of the Queen's Men. Tarlton died in 1588, and their greatest draw was gone, just as Alleyn enacting Marlowe provided a serious counter-attraction. Alleyn had left Worcester's Men, and joined the company usually known as the Admiral's Men, their patron being Charles Howard, Second Baron Howard of Effingham, Lord High Admiral and commander of the fleet that deflected the Great Armada; subsequently Earl of Nottingham.

But for two years after Tarlton's death the London theatre companies exhibited a confusing display of shuffling, as members and resources were exchanged and pooled. At length, in 1590, an important amalgamation emerged. The Admiral's Men, with their domination of tragedy, joined forces with those of the Earl of Leicester's Men who had been under the patronage of Ferdinando Lord Strange (later the Earl of Derby) since Leicester's death. Their principal actors, Will Kemp and Thomas Pope, were comedians. This versatile company dominated the theatre for the next four years. And many of its members were to be Shakespeare's fellows.

The Prentice Writer

King Richard III

By the years 1589-90, it is generally agreed, Shakespeare was a man of the theatre and was writing his first plays. We know, from a famous pamphlet of Robert Greene's, that *Henry VI pt 3* was written by 1592. (It follows that parts 1 and 2 had previously appeared). And in 1598, a man called Francis Meres who was about to leave London for a schoolmastership and rectorship in Rutland published *Palladis Tamia: Wit's Treasury*, a collection of observations and apophthegms in which he included his opinions on the leading writers of the day, and happily listed twelve of Shakespeare's plays known

to him. (He set a minor puzzle, by referring to one called *Love's Labour Won*. He'd already listed *Love's Labour's Lost*, so it wasn't that; scholars have argued since whether any of Shakespeare's known early comedies might have been known by an alternative title.)

By 1590, then, we are sure that Shakespeare had at least embarked upon writing the *Henry VI* sequence. And then or over the next two or three years we think it probable that he wrote *Titus Andronicus*, *The Two Gentlemen of Verona*, *The Comedy of Errors* and *King John* (not necessarily in that order) and completed his Wars of the Roses series with *Richard III*. If we note that *The Taming of the Shrew* also shows signs of being one of his less mature works, and that *Love's Labour's Lost* also shows some signs of similarity to the early comedies, then we have completed our list of candidates for the work of Shakespeare's prentice period. We need only note further that a minority of scholars today are arguing for earlier dates of composition for Shakespeare's first work –pushing it back, say, to the Armada year of 1588.

The year 1590 found the combined Admiral's and Lord Strange's Men acting at the Theatre. Some of the Admiral's Men were touring the continent, but Edward Alleyn was at Shoreditch with his brother John. James Burbage had enlisted himself personally as Lord Hunsdon's man, and worked with whatever company was performing in his playhouse. And at this point his younger son Richard made his first recorded appearance in the theatre world, taking a part in the old fashioned play *The Seven Deadly Sins* which Strange's men had taken over from the Queen's Men.

Richard Burbage took a still larger part in his father's quarrel with his financial partners. Old John Brayne, the grocer brother-in-law had died in 1586. Even before his

Philip Henslowe's stepdaughter, Joan, who married Edward Alleyn. From a painting in Dulwich College.

death it had been clear that Burbage resented any interference with the running of his theatre, and while Brayne hardly claimed any theatrical skills, he did as a financier want some control over the 'gatherers' who took the receipts. This quarrel was taken up vigorously by Brayne's widow, who came to the Theatre with two friends in the winter of 1590 in an attempt to instal a soapmaker called Nicholas Bishop as gatherer on her behalf. Her sister-in-law Ellen Burbage immediately told her and her friends to leave before her son broke all their heads. James Burbage looked out from an upper window, and joined in the dispute by calling Mrs Brayne a 'murdering whore'. Like his wife, he warned that 'if my son come he will thump you hence'. And when son Cuthbert did come he did indeed deliver himself of some 'great and horrible oaths'.

It was Cuthbert's younger brother Richard, however, who proceeded to definite thumping. He picked up a broomstick and belaboured Mrs Brayne's friend Robert Milnes, who was hopefully brandishing a court order that was supposed to substantiate the widow's claims.

When Bishop the soapmaker intervened, Richard pulled his nose disdainfully, and threatened to beat him too. By the time the first actors arrived for the afternoon performance the enemy was routed, and Richard was flourishing his broomstick and re-enacting his part in their defeat.

The serious theatrical upshot of this rumpus was that it led to a split between the amalgamated Admiral's and Lord Strange's Men. John Alleyn, who saw the thumping with the broomstick, sympathised with the widow, and deferentially ('as a servant', in his own words) urged James Burbage to 'have a conscience in the matter'. Burbage, thoroughly aroused, asserted that he would defy court orders 'if there were twenty contempts and as many injunctions'. A week later, John Alleyn was sent to collect some money from Burbage that the Admiral's Men felt he owed them. Burbage refused to pay, and Alleyn remarked that 'belike he meant to deal with them as he did with the poor widow', and threatened to complain to the Admiral. Burbage lost his temper once more, and 'with a great oath' declared 'that

The title and a text page of the first volume of Holinshed's Chronicles of England, Scotland and Irelande. *This was a principal source of material for Shakespeare's history plays.*

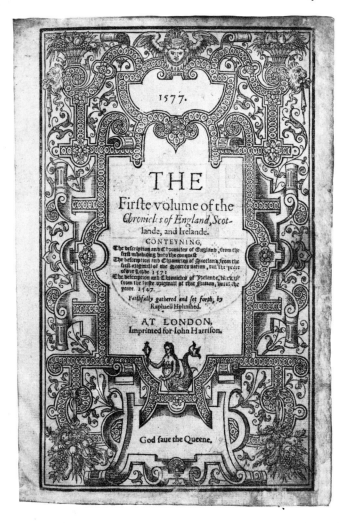

he cared not for three of the best lords of them all'. After a little litigation, the Admiral's Men made their way over to Henslowe's Rose theatre on Bankside, though Edward Alleyn followed a curious course during the next three years, retaining his personal status as an Admiral's man, but touring and acting with Strange's Men whom he probably led.

It was during this time, while Alleyn was working with the men who from 1594 onwards were certainly Shakespeare's fellows, that *Titus Andronicus* was probably written. This amalgam of Senecan horrors is by far Shakespeare's worst tragedy. It contains a dozen killings, most of them on stage. It adds multiple mutilations. Property heads, hands and stumps are much in evidence. A white empress has a black baby by her Moorish paramour: clearly Shakespeare finds this shocking, if not repulsive. And the villainous empress is finally served with a pie made from the blood and ground bones of her wicked sons.

This disgusting concoction contained a good ranting part for Alleyn as Titus. Its nauseating elements may be blamed on Seneca's influence – (his play *Thyestes*, for instance, gives the generic name 'Thyestean' to banquets whose main course is the disguised offspring of a prominent diner). Twenty years later, Ben Jonson would link this play with *The Spanish Tragedy* as examples of bad old fashioned taste. By then, no doubt, Shakespeare agreed with him. But it must have been satisfying while he was in his twenties to have his work performed by the great Edward Alleyn.

More lastingly important was the impetus Shakespeare gave to a genre for which he himself set the fashion. Since Bale's *King John*, historical tragedies had looked to the more exotic past of biblical or classical times. With the *Henry VI* sequence, Shakespeare returned to English material, and won the highest possible recognition as Christopher Marlowe immediately imitated him in *Edward II*.

The Wars of the Roses were a passage of history profoundly interesting to the Tudors. Ending only a hundred years previously, they brought within view a time of instability and near anarchy which easily persuaded Englishmen of the advantages they enjoyed in the stable Tudor dynasty. True, the religious changes effected by the dictatorial Welsh family might have made them unpopular: Henry VIII beheading his persistent Catholics, Mary lighting up Smithfield with her obstinate Protestants, and Elizabeth hanging such of Mary's surviving priests as insisted on carrying out their religious duties. Nevertheless, a glance at the last reigns of the Plantaganets showed that a secure dynasty was worth the sacrifice of some religious certainty. Throughout the sixteenth century the majority of the population always rallied round the legitimate Tudor heir – (Mary rather than Lady Jane Grey: Elizabeth

King Henry VI.

rather than Mary Queen of Scots) – and Elizabeth's ministers were always urging her to marry and bear children to secure the succession, or nominate a satisfactory Protestant heir.

Shakespeare's approach to English history was patriotic and panoramic. He took no great pedantic interest in accuracy. He was quite willing to alter a man's age for dramatic effect, or to truncate or elongate a career in the interests of plotting. At times it is hard to say whether he deliberately amalgamated characters, or misunderstood his habitual sources, the chronicle histories of Holinshed and Hall. The Englishman who takes his history from Shakespeare will obtain a very shaky knowledge of the facts.

But he will enjoy a masterly interpretative overview. A prominent feature of Shakespeare's chronicle sources was the recording of a mass of notable incidents, without necessarily organising the material to concentrate upon the doings of one individual. So the doings of a king may be related for a paragraph, and then be instantly succeeded by portents observed by some provincial citizens. Unnamed peasants enter into the narrative if their lives affect those of the great. And the chronicle structure is chronological and episodic.

All this, Shakespeare enthusiastically adopted. Unlike Marlowe, who had fixed his gaze on Tamburlaine and his lieutenants, following them from council chamber to battlefield with little relief, Shakespeare went into private rooms and gardens, city streets, seashores, black magicians' lairs, and game reserves, showing a richness of human life that spread its glow into the high affairs of state and battlefields at the centre of his trilogy. The first *Henry VI* play concentrated on the wars in France, giving an English audience the satisfaction of seeing Joan of Arc portrayed as a deceitful, immoral witch; but showing, too, how envious rancour among the English grandees led to the defeat of their true hero, Talbot, prognosticating the loss of Henry V's French conquests. The famous scene in the Temple gardens where the nobles pick red and white roses to declare their sympathies in the dispute between Somerset and York has such mythic appropriateness that the Middle Temple still grows beds of perfect red and white roses to commemorate an incident that took place only in Shakespeare's imagination.

The other two plays pursue the domestic history of the troubled times, showing in part 2 the condemnation of Humphry of Gloucester's wife for witchcraft, and his own downfall, together with Jack Cade's rising; and in part 3, the wavering fortunes of Richard of York; his death, and his sons' vengence. The trilogy ends with Richard of Gloucester, the sinister hunchback, murdering Henry VI to secure his brother Edward's throne and pave the way for his own usurpation as Richard III.

The *Henry VI* plays are rarely performed, and probably are of little interest to any but Englishmen. But their performance in England has never failed. The sweeping view of an important period of national history, the bold characterisation of the harsh, vengeful men and women pursuing supreme power, and the swirling turns of fortune, all constitute an exciting narrative whose verve compensates for its lack of profundity. The second and third parts were the first plays of Shakespeare to appear in book form, quarto volumes entitled *The First Part of the Contention betwixt the two famous Houses of York and Lancaster* and *The True Tragedy of Richard Duke of York*, issued in 1594 and 1595, being an unscrupulous pirate publisher's attempt to cash in on Shakespeare's popularity with an unauthorised and inaccurate version of his

Cranmer at the stake during the Marian persecution of the Protestants. The Wars of the Roses left the English with a preference for a stable dynasty. Mary, a staunch Catholic, was a Tudor and the people supported her claim to the throne.

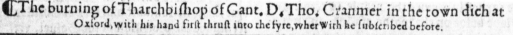

¶ The burning of Tharchbishop of Cant. D. Tho. Cranmer in the town dich at Oxford, with his hand first thrust into the fyre, wherwith he subscribed before.

L. Receiue my spirit.

Frier Iohn.

Thus haue you the full storye concernynge partes, yet be extant, and peradnenture (if God

A curious manuscript transcription of part of Titus Andronicus, *with a sketch showing a scene that never occurs in that form in the play. Titus and the Empress Tamora are in the centre: Aaron the Moor at the right. The costumes probably represent accurately Elizabethan theatrical Roman dress.*

work. It was not the last such piracy Shakespeare was to endure.

Comedy may not have come so immediately to Shakespeare. *The Two Gentlemen of Verona* is not a satisfactory play. An Italianate romantic comedy of love and friendship, it suffers from the thin characterisation of the protagonists. Valentine behaves honourably and Proteus dishonourably with too abrupt a set of responses to immediate situations on the stage. There is neither the depth nor the poetry to engage us. As the plot develops, Shakespeare proves quite incapable of surmounting the danger inherent in tragi-comic romance. He pushes before us a gallimaufry of undigested incidents and characters; scenes change as fast as characters' natures and motivations. A band of outlaws is so implausible, with their horrid personal histories and gentlemanly personal conduct, that they have quite properly been compared with the Pirates of Penzance.

But there are traces of the future Shakespeare. In Julia, who disguises herself as a pageboy to follow and win her false love, Proteus, Shakespeare first employs a theme and a technique that would recur in his later comedies. The wronged, loving woman appears, with varying emphases, in *Much Ado About Nothing*, *All's Well That Ends Well*, *Measure for Measure* and *The Winter's Tale*. The technique of disguising girls as boys would reappear with Jessica, Portia, Nerissa, Rosalind, Viola and Imogen. The device clearly had some appeal for Shakespeare: none of his contemporaries used it so habitually (or was attracted by source plots which made use of it).

Another very Shakespearean interest making its embryonic appearance in *The Two Gentlemen of Verona* is masculine friendship. Proteus's betrayal of the love and confidence existing between himself and Valentine clearly interests Shakespeare even more than his betrayal of Julia's love, and Valentine's abrupt and absurd renunciation of Sylvia ruins what was never a very promising play. But the love of man for man seems identifiable as a definite problem in Shakespeare's own life at the time when he wrote his sonnets.

The major success of the play is the character of Launce. In what may have been an addition to his already completed play, Shakespeare wrote a magnificent succession of lines for a low comedian to use in stand-up monologues to the audience. As a silent foil, Launce has his dog Crab, and Crab's manifold sins and wickednesses–failing to grieve when Launce leaves home; pissing on a grand lady's farthingale; and creating a nuisance under the dinner table–give Launce material for a steady torrent of comic grumbling. Will Kemp, the leading clown of the company, must have recognised a script writer who could do great things for him.

The Comedy of Errors is a more satisfactory work which can still entertain as a whole. It follows reasonably closely its classical source, the *Menaechmi* of Plautus, only reducing the smutty importance of the courtesan, presumably so as not to offend a bourgeois audience. The farcical consequences of two pairs of identical twins being mistaken for each other makes good, simple theatre. A touch suggesting the future greatness of Shakespeare is the introduction of the merchant Egeon, a tragic figure in danger of being hanged through no fault of his own. It would always be a feature of Shakespeare's

David Garrick as Richard III, in the eve of Bosworth scene (Act V, scene III).

Laurence Olivier as Richard III at the Old Vic, 1944.

that Shakespeare would have been able to override his prestigious senior's wishes, eschew the ranting that had brought him fame, and raise his art to the highest pitch. Burbage was a younger contemporary: the first tragic role Shakespeare created for him was the juvenile Romeo. And through the experience of younger heroes (Hal and Henry V especially) Burbage grew to the maturity of his great roles. It is possible that *King John* was written while Alleyn was still working with Strange's Men, and that in this play we see the juxtaposition of Alleyn's role as the weary old king, and Burbage's as the energetic young Bastard.

Marlowe's influence was most apparent in *Richard III*. The king who completed Shakespeare's Wars of the Roses cycle was a development of the Marlovian Machiavel. Marlowe's *Jew of Malta* had featured a wonderful figure of comic evil, exulting in his own wickedness:

As for myself, I walk abroad o' nights
And kill sick people groaning under walls.
Sometimes I go about and poison wells.

This motiveless malice fascinates, delights and horrifies simultaneously. The ignoble anti-semitism of the Turks and Christians of *The Jew of Malta* almost makes Barabas the Jew seem heroic, but his gloating malignity makes him ultimately a foreshadowing of a pantomime demon king.

Aaron the Moor in *Titus Andronicus* had shown something of this quality, but Shakespeare's own demon king carried still further the capacity for taking undisguised pleasure in his own wickedness.

I am determined to prove a villain
And hate the idle pleasures of these days,

says Richard III, as simply as he might have proposed going to market. Yet, like Barabas, he has his near-justification: the deformity that unfits him for courtly love, and sets dogs barking at his limp. Ironically, of course, the furious energy that makes him delightful to an audience also makes him plausibly attractive to women, and his ugliness and malevolence do not debar him from marrying an attractive and initially hostile victim when he chooses. Dickens understood this principle of sexual repulsion and attraction when he created Quilp.

While *Richard III* is far from being Shakespeare's best play, the role of Richard is such a splendid vehicle that actors have always kept it alive. Colley Cibber, in the eighteenth century, rewrote about half of it, and one of his interpolations was a splendid, sneery line that was long the best known in the play: 'Off with his head! So much for Buckingham!' Garrick and later Kean delighted in the role. Irving was perfectly suited to it. And it is significant that of the three Shakespearean films made by Sir Laurence Olivier, one should be of this artistically minor play with its histrionically major role.

comedy that some of the truth and the sadness of life found its place among the charm and mirth.

In 1592 Edward Alleyn took a step that would ultimately cut him off entirely from Shakespeare's company. He married Philip Henslowe's stepdaughter, and increasingly his fortunes became tied to those of the wily old financier of the Rose theatre. By leading the Admiral's Men and enjoying his father-in-law's confidence and support, Alleyn became immensely wealthy, and left in his will the money for the foundation of Dulwich College. The other Admiral's Men were kept down by Henslowe's policy of delaying wages and making loans. Henslowe and Alleyn between them enjoyed the fruits of the company's labours, whereas Shakespeare's fellows distributed their earnings more equably among themselves. But Alleyn would be remembered only as the creator of the great Marlovian roles—Tamburlaine, Faustus and Barabas, the Jew of Malta. Young Dick Burbage would enjoy the fame of creating Hamlet, Othello, Macbeth and Lear.

Since Shakespeare was a very professional writer, delivering to his actors scripts with parts suiting their talents, we may be thankful that Alleyn did go his own way. His appetite for melodrama had produced no masterpiece in *Titus Andronicus*, and we cannot be sure

'An Upstart Crow'

In 1592 Robert Greene died. His fortunes had reached a low ebb, and after a mighty carouse on Rhenish wine and pickled herrings, in the company of Tom Nashe, the satirical pamphleteer, he fell seriously ill. He was destitute, and had not a kindly shoemaker and his wife lodged him, he might then and there have died in the streets. He was attended by two women, one of whom, the mother of Fortunatus, was the sister of a notorious thief who had been hanged under the name of 'Cutting Ball'. The day before he died, Greene wrote to his deserted wife, asking her to pay the kindly shoemaker £10. After his death, the shoemaker's wife carried out his last wish, and placed a crown of bays over the red hair he had worn brushed into a fantastic quiff.

But Greene's dramatic death was not the end of him in the world of letters. In his last years he had written penitential pamphlets, sensationally confessing his own wickedness.

The last of these was published posthumously as *Greene's Groatsworth of Wit bought with a Million of Repentance*. It gave a thinly fictionalised version of Greene's early life as the story of one 'Roberto', and then broke off suddenly to address severe moral warnings to three other writers. They were not named, but there is little doubt that two of them were Marlowe and Nashe, and the third was probably Peele. All three did a little work for the players. Greene now admonished them against this, warning them that the players were mean and ungrateful. To make their ingratitude worse, now that the university men had shown them how to write plays, the wretched actors had taken it into their heads that they could do as well themselves. One of their ignorant number was actually writing! He was, however, only

> an upstart Crow, beautified with our feathers, that with his *Tiger's heart wrapped in a Player's hide*, supposes he is as well able to bombast out

a blank verse as the best of you: and being an absolute *Iohannes fac totum*, is in his own conceit the only Shake-scene in the country.

This is obviously Shakespeare. The wretched pun 'Shake-scene' and the parody of a line in which the condemned York responds to Queen Margaret's cruel taunting ('Oh, tiger's heart wrapp'd in a woman's hide', *Henry VI* pt 3, act I, sc.iv, l. 137) make this plain.

Greene's last pamphlet, published posthumously, and containing the first reference to Shakespeare as a writer and actor.

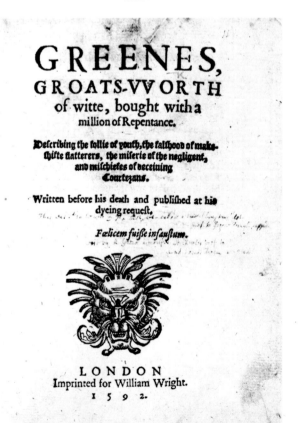

GREENES,
GROATS-VVORTH
of witte, bought with a
million of Repentance.

Describing the follie of youth, the falshood of make-
shifte flatterers, the miserie of the negligent,
and mischiefes of deceiuing
Courtezans.

Written before his death and published at his
dyeing request.

Fælicem fuiße infaustum.

LONDON
Imprinted for William Wright.
1 5 9 2.

A

QVIP FOR AN VP-
ſtart Courtier:

Or,

A quaint diſpute betvveen **Veluet breeches**
and Cloth-breeches.

*Wherein is plainely ſet downe the diſorders
in all Eſtates and Trades.*

LONDON

Imprinted by Iohn Wolfe, and are to bee ſold at his
ſhop at Poules chayne. 1 ſ 9 2.

A Quip for an Upstart Courtier: the pamphlet in
*which Robert Greene attacked Gabriel Harvey and his
brother, and so paved the way for the furious pamphlet
war between Harvey and Nashe which broke out after his
own death.*

It is a most important reference: the first, outside
parish and diocesan registers to Shakespeare's existence.
And it makes one thing clear. Shakespeare was known,
and even resented as a rising and successful writer.
Greene knew literary London and he knew the players:
he could not possibly have been mistaken or deceived
about this. He offers a guarantee, before a line of
Shakespeare's had reached print, that the works of
Shakespeare were indeed written by Will Shakespeare,
and that the great melodramatic scene in which York is
crowned with paper, tied to a stake and mocked with the
death of his son, was sufficiently well-known to be
recognised in an allusive reference.

Greene's writing gave offence. But Greene was dead,
and nothing we know about Shakespeare suggests that he
would have written an attack on a recently dead man's
memory. Instead he sought an apology from Greene's
editor. Henry Chettle was a portly stationer who had just
entered into a new partnership. He was known to have
prepared Green's *Groatsworth* for the printers, and could
be accused of inserting the offending passages. Shake-

speare and Marlowe both apparently protested, Marlowe
objecting to passages in which Greene urged him to
abandon his atheistical freethinking.

Chettle wrote his own first book in 1593. *Kind Heart's
Dream* was an exposé of some abuses of the day, but its
introductory 'Epistle' carried an explanation of his
conduct to Shakespeare:

> About three months since died M. Robert
> Greene, leaving many papers in sundry Book
> sellers' hands, among them his *Groatsworth of
> wit,* in which a letter written to divers play-
> makers is offensively by one or two of them
> taken . . . With neither of them that take
> offence was I acquainted, and with one of
> them I care not if I never be. The other, whom
> at that time I did not so much spare, as since I
> wish I had, for that as I have moderated the
> heat of living writers, and might have used my
> own discretion (especially in such a case) the
> Author being dead, that I did not, I am as
> sorry as if the original fault had been my fault,
> because my self have seen his demeanour no
> less civil than he excellent in the quality he
> professes. Besides, divers of worship have
> reported his uprightness of dealing, which
> argues his honesty, and his facetious grace in
> writing, that approves his Art.

This is no worthless testimonial. Chettle's continuing
abuse of Marlowe–he cares not if he never meets him
–shows that he was willing to stick to his (or Greene's)

*A caricature of Robert Greene writing in his shroud. His
bristling hair and beard were remembered still, six years
after his death, when this was published.*

"GREENE IN CONCEIPTE."

A sixteenth-century printing house. In the foreground a pile of new paper on the right, and printed folio formes on the left. At the press, one printer inks the type with large ink-balls, while the other removes the newly printed forme. In the background two compositors work at a double case. Each has his manuscript copy pinned up at his side, and takes letters of type from the case to go into the composing stick he holds.

guns if the offence seemed merited. But since the publication of the *Groatsworth*, Chettle had met Shakespeare, and found his manners as fine as his acting ('the quality he professes'). This is the first sounding of a note that recurs in references to Shakespeare. His 'gentleness', struck every one who met him, except Greene. Going to demand an apology for a libel, he still managed to impress the man he faced by the sheer courtesy with which he made the request. It seems to have been Shakespeare's most striking personal characteristic.

It is interesting to note that Chettle casually confirms the excellence of Shakespeare's acting. All the earliest reports of his acting praise it: it is only a later tradition,

probably reacting to the difficulty of establishing with any certainty major roles played by Shakespeare, which hints that he may not have been a leading player.

Still more interesting is Chettle's reference to 'divers of worship'. Already Shakespeare had powerful friends to speak up for him. And they spoke up under two heads. First they observed that he was honest and straightforward, as became so honourable and gentlemanly a man. Next, they confirmed from their own personal and definite knowledge that Will Shakespeare was a witty and elegant writer, so that there was no need to suppose that he borrowed his artistry from Greene.

Who, one wonders, were these 'divers of worship'? Shakespeare was soon to show the world that he had a noble patron, but would a vain young courtier have bothered to step into the disputes of tradesmen? Clearly something about Shakespeare's personality was capable of enforcing respect and concern. His own 'worship' (or public prominence) could not have enforced any important public support at this time. Somewhere, he had powerful friends.

Plague, Patronage, Poems

IN JUNE 1592 there occurred an outbreak of plague sufficiently serious to compel the authorities to close the theatres. This had not happened for five years, and may have been the first time that Shakespeare was made forcibly aware of the real physical restraint to which his profession was subject. It proved a long as well as intense visitation. 11,000 people died in 1593, and the play-houses were virtually kept closed until May 1594. Edward Alleyn was licensed by the Privy Council to tour, in company with Strange's leading Men, Will Kemp, Thomas Pope, John Hemmings, Augustine Phillips and George Bryan. Not for another year would Shakespeare's name be inscribed in this exalted company, and we do not know whether he toured with them at this time or not.

But it seems most likely that he devoted the enforced rest from playing in London to cultivating the favour of the young Earl of Southampton, and writing the two long narrative poems that he dedicated to him. In April 1593, Richard Field, a Stratford man who had been in the printing trade in London since 1579, printed his fellow Stratfordian's *Venus and Adonis*. He produced a good and careful copy, and included the author's letter of dedication:

To the Right Honourable
Henry Wriothesly, Earl of Southampton,
and Baron of Titchfield
Right Honourable,

I know not how I shall offend in dedicating my unpolished lines to your Lordship, nor how the world will censure me for choosing so strong a prop to support so weak a burden. Only, if your Honour seem but pleased, I account myself highly praised; and vow to take advantage of all idle hours, till I have honoured you with some graver labour. But if the first heir of my invention prove deformed, I shall be sorry it had so noble a godfather, and never after ear [plough] so barren a land, for fear it yield me still so bad a harvest. I leave it to your Honourable survey, and your Honour to your heart's content, which I wish I may always answer to your own wish, and the world's in hopeful expectation.

Your Honour's in all duty,
William Shakespeare.

Formal, complimentary, elaborate and stiffly presented for publication, this is nonetheless one of the only two letters by Shakespeare to survive. The other is the equally public dedicatory epistle to *The Rape of Lucrece*, printed by Field a year later, and evidently representing the promised 'graver labour':

To the Right Honourable
Henry Wriothesly, Earl of Southampton
and Baron of Titchfield

The love I dedicate to your Lordship is without end; whereof this pamphlet without beginning is but a superfluous moiety. The warrant I have of your Honourable disposi-tion, not the worth of my untutored lines, makes it assured of acceptance. What I have done is yours, what I have to do is yours, being in part all I have, devoted yours. Were my worth greater, my duty would show greater: meantime, as it is, it is bound to your Lordship, to whom I wish long life still lengthened with all happiness.

Your Lordship's in all duty,
William Shakespeare.

What do we learn about Shakespeare from these two pieces of formality? First, that he did indeed bow to the demands of formality. He was not alone in writing unctuous dedications to more or less cultivated aristo-crats, but there was a certain leeway permissible even to

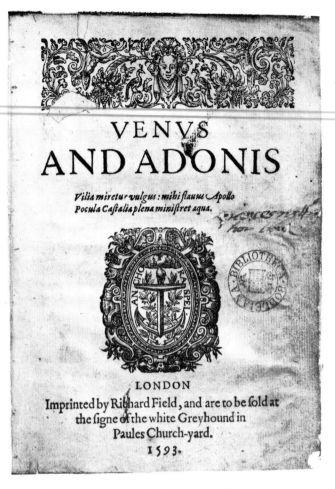

Shakespeare's first publication, the erotic Ovidian poem
Venus and Adonis, *printed by his fellow-Stratfordian,*
Richard Field.

rule could be profitably replaced by those trained to build their own fortunes, or that the chivalric tradition of *noblesse oblige* could be sensibly replaced by the pragmatic traditions of the non-aristocratic classes. And he probably believed that it was the will of God that hereditary ruling classes should rule. An ambitious man from the lower orders must be content to achieve financial security, to acquire some polish from association with the nobility, and to gain for himself recognition as one of the petty gentry. This seems to have been Shakespeare's personal social strategy.

The notice of a well-born stripling, then, was something Shakespeare cultivated assiduously as he approached thirty. The formal offer of the 'first heir of [his] invention' seems to have been satisfactory, for there is less formality and more warmth in the second dedication. His reference to the 'warrant' he has of the Earl's 'honourable disposition' clearly indicates that he had accepted some gift in return for the first dedication.

We must be clear that personal favour and advancement was Shakespeare's motive in courting Southampton. There was nothing dishonourable in following such a route to Elizabethan success: the court itself was the apex of society. 'Courtiers' were by definition and occupation men who sought favours for themselves and dispensed favours to those clients who courted them. Human frailty naturally means that such a system lends itself to toadying, factionalism, and bitter accusations of ingratitude. Courtiers, like lawyers, have always been targets of satire. But in the 1590s it was still the men rather than the system that might be criticised, and Shakespeare was doing nothing mean in seeking either a valuable gift or honourable employment from a young courtier whose own prestige would be increased by a train of satisfied clients.

According to Sir William Davenant, Shakespeare was so far successful in his appeal to Southampton that he received a gift of £1,000 to make a purchase 'he had a mind to'. The sum is preposterously large, and there is no evidence that Shakespeare ever spent so much money in a single purchase or investment. But a gift must have followed the dedications, and it may have been with capital from Southampton that Shakespeare bought his way into full membership of the theatrical company in which he appeared after the plague had ended.

Yet if Shakespeare did use his gift to secure his professional standing, this closed another avenue of advancement. To be an actor was to be a man with a recognised and socially quite humble employment. To be the mere hanger-on of a nobleman was socially superior. It is possible that Shakespeare hoped to become a part of Southampton's household, the member of his casual retinue who happened to write poems for him. The Italian John Florio who had been the Earl's tutor was passing his life as just such a hanger-on, maintaining

the Elizabethan writer, and Shakespeare does not appear to have wished to take advantage of it.

Southampton was nine years younger than Shakespeare; just twenty at the time of the *Venus and Adonis* dedication. But Shakespeare gives total respect to the social distance between them, stressing Southampton's superiority, and only glancing at his juniority in the complimentary observation that the world has a 'hopeful expectation' of him.

Shakespeare was, in fact, of conservative temperament. Though he sprang from the trading middle classes, and might have adopted a sturdy resistance to feudal relics, he preferred not to do so. His plays already showed little respect for the commons, plebeians serving as mere acclamation-fodder for Titus Andronicus, and Jack Cade's rebels being shown as a ridiculous rabble in the hands of illiterate demagogues. Shakespeare never showed any sign of thinking that aristocracy meant less than its etymology implies, 'government by the best'. He was not a fool. He knew that there were inferior and evil men among the aristocrats. But he did not think that moral qualities improved as one travelled down the social system. He did not think that those educated to

a personal reputation as the author of an Italian dictionary and the translator of Montaigne, but at Southampton's beck and call to settle disputes with the servants of other noble families. If Shakespeare did aspire to such a situation (and we may infer from some of the characterisation in comedies of the mid-1590s that it was not without its appeal for him) then he was fortunate in escaping it. His own later creation of Poins and Sir Toby Belch shows some awareness of the more or less stylish emptiness consequent upon such a parasitical life.

And in 1593 just such an empty life-style tragically ended the career of Kit Marlowe. Since the plague, he had been living at Scadbury, the Chislehurst estate of Thomas Walsingham, his old government employer's brother. For this patron he was writing the homosexually tinged, erotic poem *Hero and Leander*, not unlike the *Venus and Adonis* that engaged Shakespeare at the time. He was summoned away from this rural idyll by the Privy Council. They had been examining Marlowe's old room-mate Thomas Kyd, who was suspected of having written pamphlets fomenting hatred against immigrants, and in the course of the investigation found some blasphemous and atheistical pamphlets in his room. Kyd, clearly terrified, insisted that they were Marlowe's, and so Marlowe was directed to lodge himself within reach of London, in case the Privy Council chose to interview him on any given day.

At 10.00 a.m. on 30 May 1593, four men came into Dame Eleanor Bull's tavern at Deptford. They took a private room, and had their mid-day meal sent up. They passed the day there and in the garden, never mingling with the other customers in the ordinary. At 6.00 p.m. they were still there, and had their supper sent in to them. After supper there was some disturbance in their room, and it transpired that one of the four, a man named Ingram Frizer, was cut about the head. Another, Christopher Marlowe, lay dead upon the bed, with a deep wound through his eye made by Frizer's dagger.

The story told by Frizer was upheld by his companions, and accepted at the subsequent enquiry. He said that after supper, Marlowe had lain down on the bed while the other three sat on a bench with their backs alongside the bed, playing backgammon. While they played they discussed the reckoning for supper, and Marlowe – by all accounts an impetuously quarrelsome man – lost his temper. Frizer suddenly felt himself being beaten over the head with his own dagger, which had been hanging from his belt over the bed. Fearing for his life, as he was trapped between the bed, the back-gammon table and his companions, he swung round and forced the knife away from him, and in so doing accidentally killed Marlowe.

Anti-theatrical Puritans were only too delighted to hear that a wicked, atheistical playwright had died in a brawl in a common tavern, and they had soon exaggerated the occasion into a quarrel over a loose woman. Enemies of both Marlowe and the theatre, in fact, cannot be acquitted of having gloated abominably over his death. At the risk of seeming to join the gloating, however, we must notice that leading the 'gentlemanly' life of an aristocrat's retainer had brought Marlowe into distinctly dubious company: the kind of company that William Shakespeare entirely escaped by becoming a professional actor.

Ingram Frizer was a business agent of Thomas Walsingham's, and ended his life as a churchwarden. But he was also a skilled confidence trickster, who abused his position as Walsingham's agent to defraud innocent people of their savings. The other two men at Eleanor Bull's that day were certainly no more respectable. Robert Poley had been a more serious cloak-and-dagger man than Marlowe: a double-agent so deeply insinuated

Henry Wriothesley, Earl of Southampton, the patron who received Shakespeare's narrative poems. Believed by many to be the 'Fair Youth' of the Sonnets. Notice his effeminate hair style, and the love-knots at his waist.

The dedication of Venus and Adonis.

The dedication of The Rape of Lucrece.

in the Babington Plot (on behalf of Mary Queen of Scots) that he was lucky to be neither assassinated nor executed. The third man was, in the eyes of the local authorities, even more suspect, as he was masterless. This meant that they took him for a cutpurse – the normal occupation, in their view, of these shiftless household gentry who lost their patrons. Nicholas Skeres, as this man was named, later found himself a most distinguished patron: the Earl of Essex.

If Shakespeare had died at the same time as Marlowe, he would have held the lower position of the two in the annals of literature. In *Hero and Leander* Marlowe had given an easier flow to his heroic couplets than he employed in his theatrical blank verse. The Ovidian love poetry both poets were writing in 1593 was popular with young gallants, being both ornate and sexy. *Hero and Leander* and *Venus and Adonis* were both frequently reprinted over the next ten years. It was this lush poetry that led young men of fashion to praise '*sweet* Master Shakespeare'.

The Rape of Lucrece was a more heavy and less successful exercise in a similar vein. *Venus and Adonis* is really erotic comedy – chaste masculinity narcisistically resisting the temptations of Venus herself. Adonis is never real enough for us to feel deeply the tragedy of his death. When at the end of the poem, we are told of Venus 'Thus weary of the world, away she hies', the sense of brushing off a pretty, but inconsequential incident is acceptable. *The Rape of Lucrece* by contrast is erotic tragedy: the violent ravishing of female chastity. When, after Tarquin's heavy-breathing crime, Lucrece confesses to her husband and stabs herself, the mere prettiness of the description of her blood welling from her breasts jars against the apparent seriousness of the purpose. But the young Elizabethan reader was not to be deterred from enjoying his sweets, and *The Rape of Lucrece* went through almost as many editions as *Venus and Adonis*.

With two such successes in the courtly Ovidian mode on his hands, and quite probably some of his sonnets circulating in manuscript among fashionable readers, Shakespeare could now change his career if he chose. He might abandon the vulgar theatre, and the servingman status of being one of Worcester's or Pembroke's or Sussex's or Derby's 'Men', and become instead the more intimate associate of his individual patron. Non-dramatic verse was more socially acceptable than plays, just as it was more gentlemanly to circulate work in manuscript than to sell it to the printing-houses. If immediate social standing were really of the highest importance to Shakespeare, then, we should expect to find him becoming the household intimate of the Earl of Southampton. Yet after the publication of *The Rape of Lucrece* there is no further hard evidence of any association between them. And, indeed, the two dedications are the only conclusive evidence we have that there was any acquaintance at all between the two.

Who was this nobleman, who might so easily have become Shakespeare's 'loving lord'? Henry Wriothesly (pronounced Rizzly) was a rather silly young Catholic peer, who seemed to be making the least of the opportunities his birth offered him. His grandfather had founded the family fortune in the days of Henry VIII. His father had been mixed up in treasonable activities at the beginning of Elizabeth's reign, and died young. After some negotiation, Henry became the ward of Elizabeth's powerful minister Lord Burghley, a splendid Protestant protector for the noble boy whose name was clouded by his father's Catholic folly.

Burghley was quite willing to undertake the wardship of young aristocrats. He had successfully married his daughter to a noble ward, and now he had three granddaughters for whom he wanted distinguished husbands. In his mind, Southampton was marked down as the future husband of Lady Elizabeth Vere, his eldest granddaughter. He had Henry suitably educated at Cambridge and Gray's Inn, and in 1590, when Henry was seventeen and Lady Elizabeth fifteen, Burghley thought the marriage might be arranged. But Henry temporized. Despite his mother's anxious encouragement, he had no wish for an arranged marriage and an alliance with his politically brilliant but unglamorous guardian. Foolishly he drifted away from the centre of political power, and came more and more under the influence of the Earl of Essex, Elizabeth's last personal favourite, but a courtier whose impolitic impetuosity and ambition made him effectively leader of the opposition to her government.

Unlike Burghley, Essex had no farseeing vision of England's position in Europe, nor did he consider seriously the means by which domestic stability might be ensured. He relied upon his personal charm and good looks to win followers, and gathered to his side a dangerous faction of the disgruntled and discontented. Far too many names from the Essex circles were to turn up among the Gunpowder Plotters of the next reign.

Southampton rose high in Essex's coterie by virtue of his rank. Like Essex himself, he had little else to recommend him, and relied on charm and good looks as a substitute for intelligence. He had rather effeminate beauty, which he emphasised by wearing his hair at much more than shoulder length, and sweeping it forward in a heavy lock over his left breast. He was a willing patron of poetry: Barnabe Barnes and Thomas

Sir William Davenant, the cavalier poet and theatre manager, who was probably Shakespeare's godson, and was apparently not averse to being thought his natural son.

Lord Burghley, Elizabeth's minister.

Mary, Countess of Southampton. Her second marriage, to Sir Thomas Heneage, is believed by some to have been the occasion for the presentation of A Midsummer Night's Dream.

with a group of rather silly, idle young nobles, and beautifully catches the indolent charm of their banter. It bears all the marks, too, of being a coterie piece, written for the delectation of just such a group as it portrays. It is full of obscure, topical, satirical allusions, many of which now defy certain identification.

Lying at the heart of the play is a sketch of the situation of a man of real wit and intelligence in the court where his intellectual inferiors are lazily confident of their social superiority. This picture of Berowne, with his love for the unfashionably dark Rosaline, has long been seen as a possible self-portrait by Shakespeare. And we have no indication of any aristocratic circle but that of Southampton in which he might have experienced such elegant frustration.

Another play with which a Southamptonian connection has been mooted is *A Midsummer Night's Dream*. Written in the mid-1590s, the play's chosen setting of Theseus and Hippolyta's wedding festivities strongly suggests that it may itself have been intended to grace a patron's noble wedding. Enthusiasts for the closest possible tie between Shakespeare and Southampton have noticed that the Earl's mother married for the second time (to Sir Thomas Heneage) in 1594, and propose this as the occasion of the play. But a more widely favoured guess is that the play celebrated the nuptials of William, Earl of Derby in 1595. He was the brother of the players' old patron Lord Strange. And, even more coincidentally, he married that Lady Elizabeth Vere who had been intended for Southampton five years earlier.

In any case, it must be stressed that however much the style of the plays of the period suggest that Shakespeare had increased his association with the aristocracy, this conclusion remains a speculative inference. To go further, and build an association between Shakespeare and Southampton upon that is to remain in a field where there is no absolute certainty. We are sure that Shakespeare dedicated two poems to the Earl, and Davenant said he was paid ridiculously well for this service. That is what we know.

Nashe both dedicated collections of poems to him. It may be significant that Shakespeare's and Barnes's poems for Southampton were erotic, and Nashe's were indecent manuscript verses.

The plays of the mid-1590's suggest that Shakespeare was associating with some circle of more gentlemanly breeding than any available to him at Stratford or Shoreditch. His earliest comedies had not given any very convincing pictures of aristocratic circles, but *Love's Labour's Lost* – one of the most rewarding plays to see in performance, but one of the least satisfactory to read without an awareness of its effect when staged – deals

The Sonnets

In 1609 THOMAS THORPE published a volume entitled *SHAKESPEARES SONNETS*. It contained 154 sonnets and a longish (47 stanza) poem called *A Lover's Complaint*. The book was not nearly as carefully proof-read as *Venus and Adonis* and *The Rape of Lucrece* had been in their first editions, from which we infer that Thorpe had not Shakespeare's permission to publish: poets are particularly touchy about having their work reproduced accurately. But the book provides a definite terminal date: the sonnets were obviously written by 1609.

Some, at least, had been written a good ten years earlier and more. Francis Meres's *Palladis Tamia* recorded in 1598 that Shakespeare's 'sugar'd sonnets' were circulating in manuscript, and though 'sugar'd' is a peculiarly inept description of these particular poems, they are likely to have been around for some time before Meres could have heard of them.

The publication of Sidney's *Astrophel and Stella* in 1591 was the signal for a sudden vogue of sonneteering. Sequences were published over the next seven years by Samuel Daniel, Thomas Watson, Barnabe Barnes, Thomas Lodge, Giles Fletcher, Henry Constable, William Percy, Michael Drayton, Edmund Spenser, Richard Barnfield, Bartholomew Griffiths, William Smith, Henry Lok, Robert Tofte, and Nicholas Breton. Since no sequences were published in England before 1591, it is generally assumed that Shakespeare's was composed after that date, and comprised part of the fashionable flood between 1592 and 1598. But the possibility that manuscript imitation of Sidney's manuscript sonnets took place before 1590 cannot be ruled out.

The sonnets themselves offer no certain evidence of a date of composition. There are definite clues, but they are, unfortunately, of almost baffling obscurity, and the best of them seem to point to dates outside the 1592-98 time-span!

The most important references to the outside world at the time of composition come in sonnet 107, in which the poet predicts that his love will prove immortal, compares the impossibility of predicting its end with the failure of certain dismal prognostications made for that year, and accepts a moment of guaranteed political peace as a good time to write of love. The key lines are:

> The mortal moon hath her eclipse endur'd,
> And the sad augurs mock their own presage,
> Incertainties now crown themselves assur'd,
> And peace proclaims olives of endless age.

The 'mortal moon' of the first line needs interpretation: until we have decided who or what it is, we cannot be sure whether its 'enduring' an eclipse means it has survived or succumbed to a threat of extinction. The other three lines mean, literally, 'the pessimistic prophets are now laughing at their own former gloomy predictions; things that were dubious in prospect are now crowned with certainty, and peace declares that its olive branches shall last for ever'.

Who or what is 'The mortal moon'? The most favoured candidate is Queen Elizabeth herself. As a virgin ruler and a woman who enjoyed the hunt she was, poetically, a votaress of Diana, Roman goddess of virginity, hunting and the moon. Like the moon, Elizabeth dominated her sky: unlike Diana, however, she was not immortal.

It would, then, be very fitting to see the 'eclipse' as the great queen's death. The gloomy prophets become those who feared that civil disputes would break out as soon as she died, or that her successor would prove incompetent. They have been proved wrong by the peaceful succession (and 'crowning') of James I. And James's pacifistic foreign policy – centuries before its time – will ensure an era of peace. This is easily the most convincing of the cases made for dating the sonnet by its internal references.

The snag is that it puts it rather late: outside the 1592-

98 span suggested by the wave of sonneteering. Elizabeth died in 1603. Clearly this is a possible date for some of the sonnets. But some must have been written five years earlier, for Meres to have heard of them. And by 1603, the fashion for writing sequences was over.

Is there a suitable year between 1592 and 1600, then, that would suit sonnet 107? 1596 has been proposed. It was the year of Elizabeth's 'grand climacteric' – the ninth of those supposedly critical years which, falling at seven-year intervals, were believed to be the occasion of important changes in the body, and perhaps the fortune. The sixty-third year was supposed to be of the greatest importance, and the queen had, in fact, survived an alarming illness. One Abel Jeffes had prognosticated a dangerous sea-battle for the year, and this had not transpired. And a new agreement was negotiated with Henri IV, retaining him as an ally in the war with Spain. But none of this seems peculiarly convincing. It all falls within the range of possibility, yet it all lacks the appealing appositeness of the 1603 correlations.

Another ingenious proposal takes us into an unsuspectedly early year. It has been suggested that the 'mortal moon' was the Spanish Armada, 'mortally' dangerous to England, and sailing in a crescent formation. The Armada year (like 1603) was another of Elizabeth's climacteric years. But some of the sonnets lament the poet's increasing age, and his notoriety as a base and common player. If the Armada year was the year of their composition, then he was a very tired old twenty-four year old, and was disgusted with his profession some years before any other evidence of his success in it appeared.

At all events, we are considering a widish span of years by now: from 1588 or thereabouts at the earliest till 1603, or even a little later. There is a statement in Sonnet 104 that the poet has known the addressee for three years. This does not mean that the sequence must have been an exact three years in the writing. But it is likely enough that the sonnets were being written over a period of some years.

What, then, was this sequence like? The last two sonnets may be dismissed first. They are variants of a traditional classical conceit, playing with the idea of sleeping Cupid's arrow being dipped by a virgin into water which forms a healing bath, but proves unable to cure love. They have no connection with any other part of the collection.

The remaining 152 sonnets are felt by most readers to deal with some real passage or passages in Shakespeare's emotional life. Sidney's sequence had dealt, under fictionalized names and in conventionalized terms, with the genuine passion he felt for Penelope, Lady Rich: a passion that remained frustrated as both were married. Most subsequent sonnet cycles also celebrated one lady, either real or imaginary, but usually under some such

classical pseudonym as 'Idea'. And most used, as Sidney had done, elements of the Petrarchan tradition of blaming the frustrated passion on to the lady's 'cruel' chastity or lack of feeling.

Shakespeare is unusual in proffering no names at all in his sequence. Nor does he complain in any simply conventional way of being rejected. But in one respect he is absolutely unique. Throughout the first 126 sonnets, whenever the addressee is referred to in such a way that his sex can be distinguished, it is clear that he is a man.

Almost every one who writes on Shakespeare today spends a good deal of time insisting that friendship was unusually close between Elizabethan men; that there was nothing unusual in a slightly older man feeling profound devotion to a beautiful youth of superior social rank; and (what is true) that there is nothing in the sonnets to suggest that a physical relationship between Shakespeare and the 'Fair Youth' was ever consummated. It is further pointed out (quite correctly) that there is substantial evidence in Shakespeare's writing – notably in Sonnets 126-152 – that he was acutely alive to the sexual attraction of women. And it is observed that he did not dwell lovingly on masculine beauty in his writing, as Marlowe did. There is, in fact, a loud,

---

Thomas Thorpe's edition of Shakespeare's Sonnets.

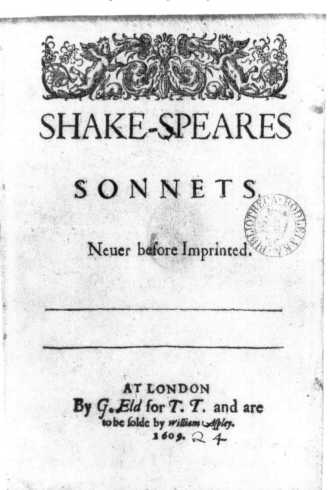

SHAKE-SPEARES

SONNETS.

Neuer before Imprinted.

AT LONDON
By G. Eld for T. T. and are
to be solde by William Apsley.
1609.

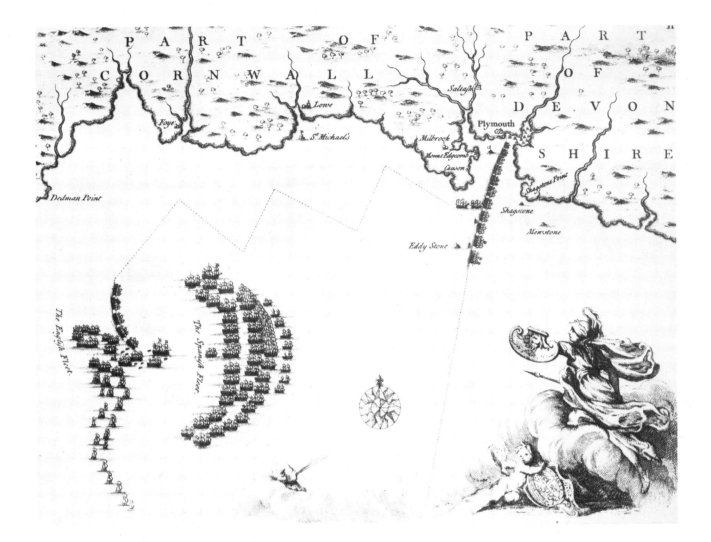

Map labels visible: PART OF CORNWALL, PART OF DEVON SHIRE, Saltash, Plymouth, Lowe, St. Michaels, Milbrook, Mount Edgcomb, Causon, Foye, Shagstone Point, Shagstone, Menstone, Dedman Point, Eddy Stone, The English Fleet, The Spanish Fleet

The English fleet putting out against the Spanish Armada, which sails in a crescent formation – thus giving rise to speculation that this was the 'mortal moon' of Sonnet 107.

defensive chorus of scholarship, of very varying quality, desperately asserting that Shakespeare was not, could not have been, must not be considered, homosexual. Rare indeed is a cool voice like that of Northrop Frye, who concludes of the sonnets that 'pederastic infatuations with beautiful and stupid boys are probably very bad for practicing dramatists'.

'Pederastic infatuation' sums up very well what confronts us in the sonnets. No amount of hot air about Elizabethan friendship can evade the fact that no other Elizabethan wrote a long sequence of sonnets to a boy. The next publisher after Thorpe to pirate the sonnets was John Benson in 1640, and he thought the property dubious enough to change some of the pronouns, so that he seemed to be printing a sequence to a girl. So it was assumed to be until eighteenth-century scholars revealed the truth they had uncovered in the first edition, whereupon eighteenth-century readers roundly expressed their disgust. Being neither in the grip of a Bardolatry that believed Shakespeare could do no wrong, nor tolerant of a practice their religion condemned, they asserted that the sonnets represented a deplorable passage in his writing. The nineteenth century started the practice of scholarly evasion. Many Victorians, too perspicacious to overlook the homoerotic

tone, tried to persuade themselves that the whole sequence was written as a series of technical exercises, so that, however distasteful the subject matter, the Swan of Avon could not be accused of depravity outside his imagination. It has remained for the twentieth century to cut the Gordian knot by blandly denying the obvious.

It must, of course, be conceded that poetic exercise is a bare possibility. Clearly the final two Cupid sonnets are just that. But there is a distinct difference in tone between these formal pieces, polishing and improving the same idea, and those sonnets which seem to deal with emotional experience.

> The little Love-god, lying once asleep,
> Laid by his side his heart-inflaming brand,
> Whilst many nymphs that vow'd chaste life to
> keep
> Came tripping by.

That is the voice of Shakespeare writing a formal exercise. And here he turns an elaborately formal sequence of the seasons in one of the personal poems.

                    Three winters cold
Have from the forests shook three summers'
                                          pride,
Three beauteous springs to yellow autumn
                                          turn'd
In process of the season have I seen,
Three April perfumes in three hot Junes
                                          burn'd
Since first I saw you fresh, which are yet
                                          green.

I have tried to be fair, and to pick as formal and exercise-like a passage as possible from the sonnets addressed to the Fair Youth. But I think that a deeper seriousness and more intense engagement, as well as finer poetry, are immediately apparent.

It is very likely that most readers who encounter the popular and often anthologised Sonnets 18 'Shall I compare thee to a summer's day' and 116 'Let me not to the marriage of true minds/Admit impediment' assume that they are about heterosexual love. But sonnets just as intense and lovely are unquestionably addressed to the young man: Sonnet 40, for example, 'Take all my loves, my love, yea take them all.' In Sonnet 20 Shakespeare makes a bawdy pun to assert that the young man is ·physiologically designed to be of no use to him – ('prick'd out for women's pleasure'). Yet in the same sonnet he praises his 'woman's face with Nature's own hand painted,' calls him 'the master mistress of my passion', and claims his love while relinquishing his 'love's use' as a 'treasure' for women.

The 126 sonnets addressed to the young man are not an exact, single sequence. Rather they seem to fall into varying groups of varying lengths. The first seventeen all revolve around the theme that the young man ought to marry and have children. There follows a short group contemplating the effects of time on the poet and the youth. A pair of sonnets play with the ideas of acting and painting as related to Shakespeare's love: another pair compares the poet's love with that of a vassal and an ambassador. In the course of the sequence we find the poet on a journey. We find him grieving that his 'motley' calling as an actor makes him unworthy of the young man's love, and noting that he cannot be publicly acknowledged by the young friend whose social position is so much higher than his own. It becomes clear, too, that at some stage the Fair Youth has stolen his friend's mistress, and in Sonnet 40 Shakespeare yields her, forgives the 'gentle thief', and concludes abjectly, 'Kill me with spites, yet we must not be foes.'

The only thing in which the poet takes a consistent pride is his belief that his work will outlive all other memorials and preserve the youth's beauty for posterity. Unfortunately it seems that other poets are claiming the young man's attention. One in particular, distinguished by 'the proud full sail of his great verse' actually succeeds Shakespeare in the young man's favour, and a handful of poems lament the ending of the Fair Youth's love for the sonneteer. But others celebrate their reunion after a separation. Two note the grace with which the young man makes his immoral life seem attractive. And the predominant theme of the last group is Shakespeare's rather melancholy declaration of his love's permanence.

George Eld's printing house undertook the production of the volume. After Sonnet 126, the printers left a space equivalent to three or four lines of type before setting the number 127 and the next poem. All the other sonnets in the volume are printed right up against each other, separated only by the lines containing the sonnet numbers. It looks as though the manuscript handed to the printers supports our impression that the first 126 sonnets are a group, and the next 26 should be examined separately.

Of this group, all but two are addressed to a woman. The two odd ones deal with abstract themes, and are justly famous. Sonnet 129 'Th' expense of spirit in a waste of shame' is a bitter outpouring of disgust at satiated lust. Sonnet 146 'Poor soul the centre of my sinful earth' is a meditation upon time, death and immortality.

There are, then, twenty-four sonnets addressed to a woman. Only two of them are straightforwardly complimentary. Sonnet 128 'How oft when thou my music music play'st' is a charming description of the beloved playing the virginals while the poet envies the keys that can kiss her fingers. Sonnet 145 'Those lips that Love's own hand did make' is an odd one that may well have no connection with the others.

The other twenty-two are astonishing love poems by any standard. At the very least, they make an extra-ordinary fuss over the fact that the lady has an unfashionably dark complexion. (Shakespeare never actually calls her a 'Dark Lady'; but she is 'a woman colour'd ill', and the blackness of her hair and, more especially, her eyes, are repeatedly stressed.) In Sonnet 130 'My mistress' eyes are nothing like the sun' he runs through a full catalogue of her attributes – eyes, lips, breasts, hair, cheeks, breath, voice and gait – finding an unfavourable comparison or negativing a traditional compliment for each. Several sonnets stress that the poet is not blinded by love to the extent that he cannot see his mistress's lack of acceptable beauty. Several others say that she is, moreover, vicious: that her black colouring aptly reflects her black soul. She has broken her 'bed-vow'; her sexual appetite is inordinate, and she compels the poet to join her in sin, as he lies by calling her beautiful. Altogether, this deceitful adulteress sounds just such an intriguing siren as might force the despairing Sonnet 129 from a sensitive man who could not tear himself from her bed.

But six of the sonnets tell a yet more lurid story of her. She is betraying the poet with a fair young man whom he

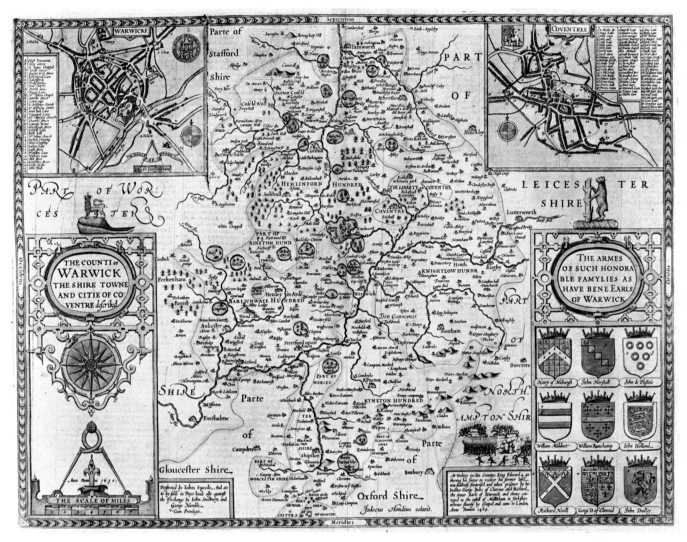

John Speede's map of Warwickshire (1610) clearly
shows the prominence of Stratford and identifies its major
feature, the bridge over the Avon. To the north, and a
little west, lies Snitterfield, birthplace of John
Shakespeare; further north still lies Henley-in-Arden,
whose name identifies the old forest region from which
William Shakespeare's mother derived her maiden name.
Temple Grafton, domicile of the mysterious and probably
non-existent Anne Whately, lies due west of Stratford;
perhaps Anne Hathaway was staying here when she got
married.

loves. In Sonnet 146 he sums up their relation to him: the young man is his good angel, the dark woman a tempting fiend. He fears that she may infect his friend with gonorrhea. And while she eagerly pursues the younger man, the poet is left pleading to be allowed to continue his own sexual relations with her, an unhappy, unwed cuckold.

The similarity of the situation to that in Sonnets 40-42 is immediately apparent. Shakespeare the lover loses his mistress to his young friend, and meekly accepts the humiliation. It seems highly likely, since this unusual tangle of relationships is repeated in two sets of sonnets addressed to different corners of the triangle, that these are genuine personal outpourings on an incident that occurred. The oddity of the incident and the individuality of the victim-poet's response adds to our sense that this is cryptic autobiography.

If, then, we have here a passage in Shakespeare's history, the detective work may begin. The suspects have left enough traces to be given tentative descriptions: they are the Fair Youth, the Dark Lady, and (a lesser figure) the Rival Poet. All that remains is for Sherlock Holmes to tell us who they were.

The Sonnets themselves give us some apparent assistance. If it is agreed that the Fair Youth of the first group is also the fair friend of the second, then it may be taken that, like Shakespeare he was called Will. Sonnet 135 makes great play with the bawdy possibilities of the Dark Lady's having her sexual desire ('will') fed by two men called Will, who want to unite their 'wills' with hers:

> Whoever hath her wish, thou hast thy *Will*
> And *Will* to boot, and *Will* in overplus . . .
>
> Wilt thou whose will is large and spacious,
> Not once vouchsafe to hide my will in thine . . .
>
> So thou being rich in *Will* add to thy *Will*,
> One will of mine to make thy large *Will* more.

Two other sonnets also plays with the young friend's name and Shakespeare's as 'Will', and the playing is so unambiguous that it must, I think, be taken as pretty certain that the lad pursued by the Dark Lady was named Will.

His surname is not, alas, revealed with the same clarity. Since the eighteenth century it has been postulated that one line in Sonnet 20 might contain the revelation. It appears in this form and spelling in Thorpe's edition:

A man in hew all *Hews* in his controwling

and it is suggested that the italicized word *Hews* points to the name Hughes. There are, of course, many words played upon in the sonnets. Shakespeare always loved puns and quibbles. But apart from the definite 'Will' and the postulated 'Hews' they are not picked out by italics and initial capital letters.

In Sonnet 1, however, in the second line, there is a clear '*Rose*', and there are throughout the sequence far more consistent attempts to associate the Fair Youth with roses than with hues. Why, then, was not this name (perhaps gentilised to something like Rowse) proposed instead of the once-occurring Hughes? The answer lies in the famous and puzzling dedication Thorpe gave his volume which runs as follows:

TO.THE.ONLIE.BEGETTER.OF.
THESE.INSUING.SONNETS.
M^r.W.H.ALL.HAPPINESSE.
AND.THAT.ETERNITIE.
PROMISED.
BY.
OUR.EVER-LIVING.POET.
WISHETH.
THE.WELL-WISHING.
ADVENTURER.IN.
SETTING.
FORTH.

T.T.

Who was Mr W. H.? As the 'begetter' of the sonnets, ought he not to be Mr W.S.? The proposal has, indeed, been mooted that W.H. is a misprint for W.S., or perhaps W.SH. It has also been suggested that the fullstop after the H is a printer's error, and the dedicatee should be a Mr W. Hall. Beyond hopefully identifying him with a rival printer and publisher, nobody has been able to say anything about the mysterious Mr Hall's connexion with the sonnets, or Thomas Thorpe's supposed reason for dedicating the book to him.

But perhaps the person who begets sonnets is the person who inspires them, and so causes the womb of the poet's brain to conceive. And Shakespeare certainly does promise the Fair Youth eternity–both in the eternal memorial the poetry will constitute, and in the promise that he, Shakespeare, will always see the youth as young. So it is a plausible guess that the Fair Youth's initials were W.H., and as the W. fits the play on his name in Sonnet 136, so those who favour Hughes believe that the volume itself identifies at least his name.

It is on this piece of ingenious deduction that Oscar Wilde built up his fictional *Portrait of Mr W.H.*, proposing a projected boy actor named Willie Hughes, and insisting that the demand that he marry and beget children in the first seventeen sonnets referred only to the 'children' of his art–the characters he was to bring to life on the stage. Wilde himself admitted that the vitiating feature of his theory was the fact that not a shred of evidence existed to suggest that any such actor ever lived. And, of course, for all the theory's aesthetic appeal to Oscar, the objection is decisive.

Wilde's contemporary, Samuel Butler, was equally sure that the Fair Youth must have been named Willie Hughes, and found that a contributor to *Notes and Queries*

William Herbert, Earl of Pembroke.

had successfully identified seven William Hugheses living at approximately the right time, though one, the Bishop of St Asaph, was a little too old and a lot too venerable. Butler found four more: the signatory of a lease in 1630; a man who wanted to repair the church of St Mary Cray in Kent; a Shropshireman who denied Christian burial to one William Fox at Burford, and threw his body into a pigsty; and a naval sea-cook. Since nothing else was known about any of them, any of them might have been Shakespeare's friend.

Butler did not, like Wilde, find it necessary to ignore the Dark Lady completely. But he was far more interested in a nasty little incident that he deduced from Sonnets 33, 34 and 121 must have taken place, and coloured the whole nature of the sequence. In Sonnets 33 and 34, Shakespeare uses the image of a sunny day that turns cloudy to illustrate the Fair Youth's emotional waywardness. He refers to travelling 'forth without my cloak', in obvious reference to his own vulnerability to this. Butler treats these images with amazing literalness, and suggests that Shakespeare was deliberately allured by the young man's beauty into a rather cruel trap, being caught, presumably with his trunk-hose down, turned

out of doors, and exposed to the ribald mockery of the youth's friends. Butler speculates furiously that Shakespeare must have nursed eternal guilt for this misdeed, and he also dates the sonnets earlier than any other theorist (1584-88) in order to assure himself that this was Shakespeare's unnatural folly of extreme youth, and not a perversion of his maturity.

The time element in the sonnets mystery is, in fact, more important from the standpoint of the Fair Youth's youth than the poet's moral responsibility. With a plausible time span of from six to fifteen years, for the writing of the sonnets no one candidate could have retained the adolescent effeminacy that so charmed Shakespeare over the entire period. Thus those who favour Southampton as the Fair Youth are bound to believe that the sequence was written very early in the 1590s. Southampton was eighteen by 1581, and despite his lovely long hair, he had not many more years in which the girlish lips and complexion Shakespeare fancied could be expected to survive. Moreover, within a few years he had fallen in love with Essex's cousin Elizabeth Vernon, and needed no encouragement from Shakespeare to marry her: all he asked was that the Queen would grant her permission. By 1598, with characteristic incaution, he had impregnated his Elizabeth, for which he was committed to the Fleet Prison in token of Her Majesty's displeasure at such goings-on with her chaste maids-of-honour. Soon he was free and married.

What, then, is the strength of the case for Southampton? First, that he knew Shakespeare and stood in a patronal relationship to him in the 1590s. He is the only young man of whom this can be averred with certainty. Second, that his portraits show an effeminacy at least in his coiffure, which accords with Shakespeare's account of his beautiful boy. Third, that in the first years of the decade, all the Earl's mature advisers were extremely anxious that he should placate Burghley by marrying Lady Elizabeth Vere, and avoid the fine that the old man was entitled to levy on his ward's estate should he refuse to do so. In fact it cost Southampton £5,000 to get out of the marriage.

On the other hand, Southampton was named Henry Wriothesly; could *not* be one of the Dark Lady's Wills; and was unlikely to have his initials reversed into W.H. Determined Southamptonites meet this difficulty by insisting that Thorpe dedicated the volume to the person who (be)got the poems for him: the procurer of the manuscripts rather than their inseminator. And they offer an immediate candidate: Sir William Harvey, an old soldier who became the Earl's mother's third husband after her second widowing in 1598. It is, of course, a mere guess that Harvey really did have access to the manuscripts, let alone that he took the responsibility upon himself of handing them over to a not too scrupulous publisher in 1609.

*Above : Stratford-upon-Avon. The river and the bridge
built by Sir Hugh Clopton in 1490.*

*Opposite, top : An English woodland scene. Shakespeare's country
background would have included scenes like these.*

*Bottom : Holy Trinity Church, Stratford-upon-Avon, in
late sunlight. The original building dates from the
thirteenth century. Shakespeare was christened in this
church, and is buried there.*

It is sometimes claimed that external support for Fair Youth Southampton, erroneous initials and all, is provided by a curious poem called *Willobie his Avisa*. This tells of an innkeeper's wife, Avisa, rejecting numerous suitors of various nations, including 'Henrico-Willobego, Italo-Hispanensis'. The argument to this part of the poem puts forward a curious little tale with the right initials to suggest something strangely like the sonnets triangle. Part of the story runs as follows:

> H.W. being suddenly infected with the contagion of a fantastical fit, at the first sight of A, pineth a while in secret grief, at length not able any longer to endure the burning heat of so fervent a humour, bewrayeth the secrecy of his disease unto his familiar friend W.S. who not long before tried the courtesy of the like passion, and was now newly recovered of the like infection.

Later, theatrical imagery occurs, 'H.W.' being 'this new actor' in 'this loving Comedy', wherein W.S. was 'the old player'. This last image is sometimes treated as a proof that W.S. was Shakespeare. If H.W. *was* intended to stand for Henry Wriothesly, then the poem would be evidence that the Earl's sharing a mistress with the older player was a matter of common gossip.

But H.W. is far more likely to stand for Henry Willobie, the presumed author of the poem, whose name is transparently hidden under 'Henrico Willobego'. Willobie was an Oxford man. One year before he took his degree the poem appeared with an 'Epistle to the Reader' dated from Oxford and signed by one Hadrian Dorrell who claimed to have found the manuscript among his roommate's effects. Commendatory verses including a reference to Shakespeare's *The Rape of Lucrece* have been ascribed to two Balliol men of the time, and the whole thing seems more like an undergraduate prank than anything else. At present it is even less clear what lies behind *Willobie his Avisa* than what lies behind Shakespeare's sonnets. Which makes *Willobie* very bad supporting evidence for any theory.

The principal challenger to Southampton is William Herbert, Earl of Pembroke. It is obvious that the initials W.H. are now in order, and the name Will is back in place. But where did Herbert spring from as a candidate for intimacy with Shakespeare?

His name was first linked with Shakespeare's in print after the poet's death. When in 1623 the actors John Hemmings and Henry Condell prepared their former colleague's plays for the press, they dedicated the volume 'To the most noble and incomparable pair of brethren, William, Earl of Pembroke . . . and Philip, Earl of Montgomery.' And in their dedicatory epistle Hemmings and Condell volunteered the information that the two earls had enjoyed the plays so much on the stage that they were the natural dedicatees, and moreover, 'pro-

Elizabeth Vernon, cousin of the Earl of Essex, became Southampton's wife after he had made her pregnant, to the fury of Queen Elizabeth. It was as Countess of Southampton that Mistress Vernon referred to Lord Cobham and his mistress as 'Sir John Falstaff and . . . Dame Pintpot'.

secuted . . . their Author living, with . . . much favour'. It is this favour extended to Shakespeare that is the only hard evidence for a connection between Pembroke and Shakespeare, and so it is the keystone of the case for him as the Fair Youth.

When or what this favour was we do not know. It is just possible that prior to 1594, Shakespeare might have been working with Pembroke's Men, the company under the patronage of William Herbert's father. After 1594 we know that he was not. And prior to 1594, Herbert was less than fourteen years old. Unless Shakespeare is to be accused of rather alarming paedophiliac tendencies (and Herbert of remarkable precocity), Herbert as W.H. dictates that the sonnets must have been written in the latter half of the decade.

One tenuous connection emerges in 1595. In that year there were negotiations afoot for a marriage between Herbert and the granddaughter of Lord Hunsdon the Lord Chamberlain. And by that time Shakespeare was definitely a member of the Lord Chamberlain's Men, under Hunsdon's patronage. Here, it is suggested, was an occasion for the first seventeen sonnets urging the Fair Youth to marry.

A factor strongly in Pembroke's favour is his character. By all accounts he was a notable womaniser. He got into his first serious scrape when he was twenty, and his mistress, the court lady Mary Fitton, bore him a child. Like Southampton, he was imprisoned for his imprudence, and Mistress Fitton was packed off out of the Virgin Queen's outraged presence. Unlike Southampton, Pembroke did not proceed to make an honest woman of his lover. As late as the Restoration he was remembered as a notable sensualist, although his honesty in public life and his generosity as a patron of learning and the arts had added a gloss to his reputation by then. Altogether the case for Herbert as Fair Youth has proved unusually tempting to otherwise conservative and cautious scholars.

There is one point against him. He succeeded to the Earldom of Pembroke in 1601, and was a man of twenty-nine by 1609. It is extremely unlikely that an aristocrat who had passed his entire majority in a high rank of the peerage would have accepted, or Thorpe dared to inscribe, a dedication to him as plain Mr W.H. And, of course, there is no real evidence that Shakespeare even knew Herbert during the 1590s. The discovery of a man, with the right initials, of an age that might be right if the sonnets were written in one part of the available time, whose character and christian name also fit, is simply insufficient evidence for any confident assertion that the

Edmund Spenser (1552-99), a friend of the Earl of Essex and Sir Philip Sidney and, like the latter, an Elizabethan sonneteer.

identity of the Fair Youth has been ascertained.

The latest candidate for Fair Youth is again equipped with the right initials and christian name. About his sex life nothing is known, but the history of his adult life proves him to have mismanaged his money extravagantly. He forces us back into the earliest normal period for dating the sonnets – 1588-89 – and his discoverer, Leslie Hotson, ingeniously argues that the pose of advanced age was quite commonly adopted by juvenile Elizabethan sonneteers, and gives good examples of twenty-year-old poets bewailing their white hair. Clearly checked, though, by Shakespeare's evident feeling that he really was substantially older than his friend, Hotson produces the less convincing argument that no age gap is more profoundly *felt* than that between eighteen and twenty-four.

The new candidate is Mr William Hatcliffe, a student at Gray's Inn and the son and heir of a family of Lincolnshire gentlemen. Hatcliffe's sole claim to fame (apart from being Hotson's candidate for Mr W.H.) is that he was the students' Lord of Misrule at the Gray's Inn Christmas festivities of 1587-88. At the Inns of Court the student masters of the annual revels were given spoof royal titles, and went through elaborate burlesques of the rituals of Elizabeth's court. Gray's Inn's festive lord was always known as the Prince of Purpoole (a corruption of Portpool, the ancient manor upon which the Inn was built), and Hotson argues that all the references to the Fair Youth as kingly reflect Hatcliffe's state during his brief year of office.

The argument wears thin at times, notably when the first seventeen sonnets are casually explained away as a parody of the normal stately demand that a sovereign get issue to secure his succession. And he is quite unpersuasive when he denies the presence of any homoerotic tone in the writing and proffers much cooler expressions of dutiful love to royalty as supposed parallels.

Willie Hewes? One of the William Hugheses? Henry Wriothesly? William Herbert? William Hatcliffe? These are the only named candidates for the role of Fair Youth that merit any consideration. Other proposals such as Walter raleigH, or WalsingHam, or an illegitimate son of the Earl of Oxford curiously masquerading under the name of William sHakespeare can all be dismissed out of hand, as they all emerge from the hopeless and fatuous attempts to 'prove' that some one other than Shakespeare wrote his works. None of the serious candidates has convinced a working majority of scholars since the brief period of Herbert's ascendancy. Almost all serious scholars agree that any of them, or some other completely unrecognised person, *might* be the Fair Youth. There is, perhaps, a small preponderance in favour of Southampton at this moment in time. But much evidently hangs on the dating of the sonnets.

Dating is surprisingly less important in the search for

*Top : Queen Elizabeth I and some of her Knights of the
Garter – including the Earls of Huntingdon, Essex,
Derby, Pembroke and Rutland. From the engraving by
Hogenberg in the British Museum, after a painting by
Nicholas Hilliard.*

*Above : London, 1572. A map attributed to Georg
Höfnagel in* Civitates Orbis Terrarum, *in the
Guildhall Library.*

Above : This portrait in Corpus Christi, Cambridge, is believed to be a true likeness of Christopher Marlowe, but final proof has never been established. By permission of the Master, Fellows and Scholars of Corpus Christi College.

the Dark Lady. There are less intriguing clues to her identity or name in the poems, and Shakespeare's insistence that sexually she was highly experienced and far from conventionally beautiful seems to allow wide license in the matter of her age. Probably the best known name to be ascribed to her is that of Mary Fitton. Bearing Herbert's bastard made her quite immoral enough for late Victorians, and that known liaison with a candidate for Fair Youth whose stock stood very high at the time seemed to clinch it. Her unmarried state should have caused doubt: the Lady's breach of her 'bed-vow' is surely an accusation of adultery. And when at last two well-authenticated portraits of Mistress Fitton were discovered which proved her to have been fair, the case fell utterly and stonily to the ground.

An interesting name which is occasionally canvassed today is that of Lucy Morgan alias Lucy Negro alias Lucy Parker alias Black Luce. She was a well-known bawd of the 1590s, running a brothel in Clerkenwell. The students of Gray's Inn mocked at her in their Christmas revels of 1594-5, listing her among the brothel-keepers who held 'Signiories' under the Prince of Purpoole, as

> *Lucy Negro*, Abbess de *Clerkenwell*, holdeth the Nunnery of *Clerkenwell*, with the Lands and Privileges thereunto belonging, of the Prince of Purpoole by Night-Service in *Cauda*, and to find a Choir of Nuns, with burning Lamps, to chaunt *Placebo* to the Gentlemen of the Prince's Privy-Chamber, on the Day of His Excellency's Coronation.

This rigmarole of Elizabethan students' slang states that Black Lucy the bawd of Clerkenwell, holds the land and title to the brothel of Clerkenwell from the Prince of Purpoole by virtue of the service in the tail she offers by night; and she is bound to organise a choir of poxy whores who will sing out 'I'll please you' to the prince's friends when he is crowned. 'Placebo' was an authentic whore's invitation of the time.

Lucy was, of course, a white woman. The adjective 'black' simply meant dark-haired in the sixteenth and seventeenth centuries. The notion that Shakespeare had an affair with a black, mulatto or Asian woman is unfounded, however appealing.

But what on earth has this bawd, of very indeterminate age, to do with Shakespeare's educated, virginals-playing mistress? A lady of her profession might well be called 'the bay where all men ride', or hear the plea, 'Among a number one is reckoned none. Then in that number let me pass untold'. Shakespeare might well feel that she was 'Enjoy'd no sooner but despised straight', and have feared that she would 'fire out' or infect his young friend. But who in his right mind would tax a procuress with her adultery? And what evidence is there that Black Luce was ever married? The fact that she was once indicted under the name of Parker in 1600 is not

evidence that she had married a man of that name ten or more years earlier.

Leslie Hotson, who favours this candidate, equates her with Luce Morgan, one of the Queen's familiar gentlewomen between 1579 and 1581. Apart from the correspondence of names, the only evidence he has to suggest that the two were the same is the fact that Luce Morgan once received 'six yards of russet satin and two yards of black velvet', which he assumes were to match her colouring.

Another candidate has been put forward by A. L. Rowse. He has discovered one Emilia Lanier, née Bassano, who was the daughter of one of the Queen's Musicians; the mistress of Lord Hunsdon between about 1588 and 1592; the wife, from 1592, of another musician, Alphonso Lanier, who served in the Azores expedition with the Earl of Southampton. While her husband was away, Emilia became the teasing mistress of the well-known astrologer and quack, Simon Forman. And in 1611 she published a book of poems prefaced with a prose attack on men.

Since Rowse is an ardent Southamptonite, it seems to be the chance association between Lanier and the Earl that ultimately convinces him that Emilia must have been shared between Wriothesly and Shakespeare. He makes little of the association with Hunsdon as a link to Shakespeare, as Hunsdon did not take over the patronage of the Earl of Derby's Men until 1594, and it is essential to Rowse's Southampton argument that the triangular events should have taken place in 1591-2.

Mistress Lanier is in many ways a more plausible candidate than the queen of the Clerkenwell stews. Her father and husband at least were musical, so she may well have been able to play the virginals. Her marriage rescued her from an unhallowed pregnancy, the child apparently being Hunsdon's. Forman found her so maddening a tease that he called her a whore (and she was certainly deceiving her husband with him). All this fits in with Shakespeare's account of his lady.

More tenuously, being half Italian she *might* have been dark. Her attack on men in 1611 contains passages that *might* have been evoked by the furious recognition of her exposure in Shakespeare's recently published sonnets. And her poems themselves prove her intelligent, and therefore, presumably, a suitable companion for Shakespeare.

Why should we not accept that this solves the problem, and agree with Rowse that Emilia Lanier *was* the Dark Lady? Simply because, once again there is not a shred of direct evidence that Shakespeare had ever heard of the lady. Rowse has long believed that Southampton must have been the Fair Youth. Now he has built upon this speculative conviction the further speculation that a woman whose *husband* was known to the Earl must *herself* have been known to Shakespeare. It is the Mary Fitton story all over again. Scholars who are sure they know the identity of one character proceed to identify another from the acquaintances of their first choice. Rowse has discovered an exceedingly interesting early feminist for us. But he has not identified the Dark Lady.

An even remoter proposal was made fifty years ago. Richard Field, the Stratford man who printed Shakespeare's narrative poems, had a French wife called Jacqueline (*anglice* Jacklin–and perhaps Jacquinetta). Obviously, like Italian Mrs Lanier, Mrs Field must have been dark . . . And Shakespeare had to learn the French he used for his lightly risquè scene between Katherine and her attendant in *Henry V* . . . and so Jacklin Field has been proposed. And rejected. One curious thing that the darkness of Shakespeare's mistress has established is the willingness of scholars to believe that a dark complexion, a Mediterranean heredity, and sexiness are an inevitable combination!

So far we have only looked at identifications of the Lady which work on the principle of computer-dating: feed in features of known Elizabethan women, and pick the one who matches best. But there is one candidate who emerges from a quite different process. She is extrapolated from the traditions surrounding Shakespeare, and indeed has no ascertainable features to match the Lady of the sonnets.

It was gossippy old John Aubrey who noted down in the 1680s what he had heard from and of Sir William Davenant (1606-68):

> Sʳ William Davenant Knight Poet Laureate was borne in [Cornmarket] Street in the City of Oxford, at the Crown Tavern. His father was John Davenant a Vintner there, a very grave and discreet Citizen: his mother was a very beautiful woman, & of a very good wit and of conversation extremely agreeable . . .
> Mʳ William Shakespeare was wont to go into Warwickshire once a year, and did commonly lie at this house in Oxon: where he was exceedingly respected . . . Now Sʳ Wᵐ would sometimes when he was pleasant over a glass of wine with his most intimate friends . . . say, that it seemed to him that he writ with the very spirit that Shakespeare, and seemed contentended [sic] enough to be thought his Son: he would tell them the story as above, in which way his mother had a very light report, whereby she was called a whore.

Aubrey might be suspected of embroidering Davenant's enthusiastic expression of poetic kinship with Shakespeare at a time when most younger poets preferred to be numbered of the 'Sons of Ben' (Jonson). But two other independent commentators picked up gossip about Shakespeare and Mistress Davenant which they recorded in 1698 and 1709. The latter noted that it was still believed in Oxford that Shakespeare had been Davenant's godfather and might have been his natural father.

An innkeeper's wife in Oxford? We are back in the world of *Willobie his Avisa*. Was some liaison between Shakespeare and the landlord's wife of what was then known as The Tavern familiar to students? Could Jane Davenant have been both Willobie's Avisa and Shakespeare's Dark Lady?

If she was the Dark Lady, then her vicious ways and unfashionable appearance were known only to her lover. For all other accounts suggest that she was beautiful and virtuous. Willobie's Avisa, too, proved firm in her virtue, despite the opinion expressed by Mr W.S. in that poem that she 'might be won'.

We have here, in fact, local gossip long after the event. It is highly likely that Shakespeare did stay at Davenant's Tavern on journeys between London and Stratford–Sir William's brother Robert confirmed this, according to other Restoration antiquaries. He might have stood as a sponsor at the vintner's son's christening. And he may have been a suitably lively companion for Jane, whose husband, by all accounts, was a bit of a sobersides. William Davenant's birthdate (1606) is, however, a little on the late side for the publishing history of the sonnets.

The Dark Ladies are far from bringing us to a solution to the Fair Youth problem. There seem to be possibilities, but no more. Sherlock Holmes might well observe, 'The threads are almost in my hand, Watson. But I require one further piece of evidence.'

The sonnets question's almost certain insolubility coupled with its proliferation of clues make it a true historical mystery appealing to the armchair detective like no other except the attempt to identify Jack the Ripper. It is a case for Sherlock Holmes, and he should be allowed to apply his method to the area we have not looked at . . .

'It is a riddle,' he said, fixing the cloud of tobacco smoke with a keen gaze, 'but it can be solved. And the answer, Watson, must lie in the Rival Poet.'

'But surely, Holmes,' I cried, 'there are even less clues to his identity than there are to the Fair Youth and the Dark Lady! If, with all the information we have about them, we still have not succeeded in establishing their names with certainty, how can we hope to do so for this man about whom we know so little?'

'So little?' murmured my friend, as if reflecting to himself. Then, pulling himself together with a start he continued, 'Proceed, Watson. With your admirably ordered mind, help me to adjust my thinking to the problem by reminding me just what that little is.'

I began confidently, checking from time to time the notes I had made since we started on this most

*Edward Alleyn, creator of the great Marlovian roles, and
possibly of Titus Andronicus. He died the richest of all
Elizabethan actors, and founded Dulwich College.*

Above : Nonsuch Palace, in Surrey, from a painting of the Flemish School in the Fitzwilliam Museum, Cambridge. The queen was at Nonsuch when the Earl of Essex burst in on her after abandoning his command in Ireland.

Top : Sir Walter Raleigh. The handsome and accomplished courtier as portrayed by Hilliard. It was Raleigh who initiated meetings of wits and writers at the Mermaid Tavern.

fascinating of all historical cases. 'Shakespeare first mentions the problem of rivalry in Sonnet 78,' I observed, 'though at this point he is not concerned about one poet. "Every alien pen," he says, 'addresses "poesy" to the young man, and he seems to catalogue a range from ignorant novices to elegant masters who have been inspired by the Fair Youth.'

'You are being excessively cautious. The syntax, it is true, literally indicates plural novices and masters, but surely, Watson, the tone of this and the succeeding sonnets entitles us to take it that Shakespeare is modestly disparaging his own standing as a tyro, and pointing up the superior education and cosmopolitanism of the one rival who predominates in the later poems?'

'But I thought we have agreed that ——'

Holmes smiled at my embarrassment.

'You are remembering our little contretemps, Watson, when you allowed this particular sonnet to mislead us into thinking we had found not only a solution, but a namesake – perhaps an ancestor – for you. No, it is true we must not put so much weight on "alien pens" as to presume that it inevitably points to the French-born Thomas Watson. His presumptive Oxford education would make him learned, and a sonneteering style not unlike Shakespeare's might well persuade our bard to praise his grace. The less critical Meres declared Watson to be the equal of Theocritus, Petrarch and Virgil. But do not preen yourself too abruptly upon this ancestor, Watson. No one with judgement in these matters now agrees with him.'

'As I recall, Holmes,' I said rather hotly, 'it was you yourself who sent me to pursue the clues leading to Watson.'

'Yes, indeed', he replied, 'but I did not expect that even you would make such emphatic claims for a candidate whose death in 1592 limited our scope in searching for the Youth and the Lady so intensely. We may bear Thomas Watson in mind, but we must not expect too much of him.'

After a little pause, I returned to my notes.

'In Sonnet 79 Shakespeare declares that the Youth deserves "the travail of a worthier pen" than his own. In Sonnet 80 he goes further, and asserts that he is receiving it: that his own work is like a little ship which may be sunk upon the Ocean of the Youth, whereas his rival is a boat of "goodly pride", fit to float upon the deep – Why, Holmes!' I cried, 'I have it! I see why you directed attention to the Rival! It is here in this sonnet that the Fair Youth is actually identified!'

'Really, Watson?' said my friend. 'I see that the study of my method has led you somewhere. Pray tell me what you have concluded, and outline your deductive procedure.'

I was sufficiently excited to blurt out directly, 'He calls him Ocean! Shakespeare calls the Youth "Ocean"!'

Mary Fitton, expelled from court after William Herbert, Earl of Pembroke, made her pregnant. From about 1880 to 1900 she was widely believed to be the 'Dark Lady' of the sonnets.

'Well?' said Holmes, not moving.

'But don't you see? That was the nickname Walter Raleigh was always given. Because the Elizabethans pronounced Walter as "water" even the Queen called him her Ocean, and Raleigh himself used the name in a long complimentary poem to Her Majesty. Now this entire sonnet fixes upon sea-faring, which was Raleigh's great claim to fame. His wide worth could have been stressed at any time up to his brief imprisonment in 1592 – *and* he returned to moderate favour before the decade was out! And, look! Raleigh's notorious vice is tactfully transferred to the Rival Poet and turned into a virtue when he is praised for his "goodly pride". I'll stake my life on it, Holmes! Raleigh was involved in the sonnets triangle. He *was* the Fair Youth.'

Sherlock Holmes looked enigmatically at me and smiled. Then he said, 'Capital, Watson. You have used my method with your customary skill. Your train of connective evidence is quite satisfactory. But haven't you overlooked two things?'

I reached quickly to the bookshelf, took down Shakespeare's *Sonnets*, and studied Sonnet 80 carefully, while my friend drew on his fine cigar and watched me quizzically.

'No, Holmes,' I said finally, looking up. 'I have

scrutinised this sonnet carefully, and I cannot see that there is anything in it which would make me doubt that the play on "Ocean" and "water" should direct us to Raleigh.'

'What you say is quite true,' remarked Sherlock Holmes, 'and it serves perfectly to exemplify the extraordinary limitations of following puns, wordplay and supposed codes as central evidence in the historical questions surrounding Elizabethan poetry. You have just, my dear Watson, used with great skill the methods which are traditionally used to prove that Bacon wrote Shakespeare, and that have been used to argue the claims of Will Hatcliffe and Luce Morgan for Youth and Lady. And with this tool, you have proved to your own satisfaction that the Fair Youth was a man ten years older than Shakespeare and notorious for his dark complexion!'

I was dumbfounded. There was nothing to do but return the *Sonnets* to the shelf and take up my notes again.

'Sonnet 81 merely says the Youth will live in Shakespeare's verse. Sonnet 82 seems to point to Southampton, as Shakespeare hints that the Youth has passed from the book he has dedicated to him to the dedications of another poet. He also seems to say that his own poetry is plain, and the Rival's has "strained touches" of "Rhetoric". I say, Holmes, do you really think Shakespeare could have called *Venus and Adonis* "plain words"?'

'Don't you think that depends on what poetry of the Rival's he had in mind for comparison?' asked my friend. 'But what is more interesting,' he went on, 'is the way in which this Rival's presence keeps bringing us down to firm questions of time. It is quite unlike that unsatisfactory vagueness we found when investigating the Dark Lady. Notice that *if* Shakespeare is here referring to one or both his narrative poems, we must be considering a date no earlier than 1594. Marlowe ——' his eye twinkled —— '*and* Watson are then ruled out as rivals, and we are in search of a rhetorician of the later 1590s. But continue.'

'Sonnet 83 tells us that Shakespeare has not written much on the Youth recently, and so the Rival has become one of "both your Poets". Sonnet 84 says nothing specific about him. But Sonnets 85 and 86 give us the most information. The Rival has a "golden quill"; his "precious phrase" is "by all the Muses fil'd". He makes Shakespeare feel "like an unletter'd clerk". His pen is "well refin'd" "In polish'd form". He is an "able spirit", "by spirits taught to write, Above a mortal pitch" – I've forgotten what that means, Holmes. Surely there were no distilled liquors in England in the sixteenth century?'

'No, no, Watson! By all means, pour yourself a brandy if poetry makes you thirsty! But do not confuse the magic of necromancy with the heated stimulus alcohol offers a fagged brain! No, the spirits are like the "affable familiar ghost Which nightly gulls him with intelligence". Either we have a private reference here, as those aver who would assert that the affable familiar ghost of England was Puck, or Robin Goodfellow, and further assert that Robert Greene was nicknamed Robin and thought of as a good fellow, and so the Rival must have been a friend of Greene's ——'

'Nashe!' I cried at once.

'No, Watson. *Not* Nashe,' my friend replied, a little curtly. 'Pray do not impetuously put forward the first name that comes to mind as fitting any category. Almost every commentator who puts the sonnets early enough to admit of the possibility that there is reference to Greene also believes that the Rival *must* have been Marlowe.'

'Ah, of course,' I said. 'As a Cambridge man he must have been learned and he probably knew Greene there. I suppose Greene couldn't have been his own affable familiar ghost? Shakespeare saying, as it were, that he was too clever by half, or clever enough for two – something of that sort?'

'Ingenious, Watson, but highly improbable,' was the answer. 'No, few people would connect Greene with the *Sonnets* at all. Most canvassers of Marlowe's claims point firmly to his necromantic play *Doctor Faustus* as an adequate explanation for the reference.'

'But Holmes,' I interjected, 'that is like pointing to *Romeo and Juliet* to prove that the Dark Lady must have been under fourteen.'

My friend was clearly pleased. 'Admirable, Watson. You exaggerate somewhat, but you are clearly beginning to see for yourself some of the snags in this sort of theorizing. There is, however, an alternative Marlovian argument which may permit us to continue his case. Suppose that Marlowe's suspected connection with your friend Sir Walter Raleigh led Shakespeare to believe that he took part in the atheistical practices alleged against the little group of intellectuals and mathematicians known as Raleigh's "School of Night"? Might he not be suspected of necromancy among them?'

'I suppose so,' I replied. I could see that Holmes was not deeply attached to the theory, and I proceeded, 'My note observes that the strongest case for Marlowe rests upon the words, "the proud full sail of his great verse", which critics feel well describes Marlowe's mighty line.'

'Yes,' said Holmes. 'Marlowe also had the fame that the rival clearly has in Shakespeare's estimation. Those who feel that our Bard must have been as proud as a don think that only Marlowe could have led him to describe himself as inferior. For myself, however, I must voice the suspicion that Shakespeare wrote these sonnets early enough to be unsure about his own standing, and that he may have thought more highly than we do of a good many of his contemporaries.'

'You are thinking of Barnabe Barnes?' I asked in astonishment.

Robert Devereaux, 2nd Earl of Essex, in 1597. From the painting by an unknown artist in the National Portrait Gallery. He was the queen's last favourite, and the close associate and faction leader of Shakespeare's patron, Southampton.

Queen Elizabeth in her last years. An allegorical painting, c. 1600, in the possession of Lord Methuen.

'Oh dear, no! I should hardly like to postulate a theory on the strength of one dedication to Southampton, especially when we have agreed that the Earl was not inevitably the Fair Youth. No, I was thinking more of Chapman, asserted by some (on very little evidence) to have been almost the official poet of Raleigh's School of Night. He might have been linked in Shakespeare's mind with "his compeers by night", though the scholars nowadays seem determined to assert that Chapman's verse could never have been described so flatteringly by Shakespeare.'

'Do you then propose Chapman?' I asked in some surprise. It was not like my old friend to give his decisive vote to an old theory without adducing new evidence.

'Certainly not,' was the quick reply. 'I have told you, Watson, there is not at present sufficient evidence in our hands to permit us to reach a final solution. Nothing is more damaging to successful detective investigation than rushing over-hastily to a conclusion. You must recall the Case of Sir Thomas Lucy's Deer-Park.

'No, all I propose is that we keep the investigation bubbling merrily. Until fresh documentary evidence comes to hand (which it never may) we shall continue to be the sport of theorists. But that sport can be continued best if the numbers of candidates are steadily increased.

'Now, you will observe, Watson, that hitherto candidates have been unearthed in searches for noble and immoral youths initialled W.H., or dark-haired women who are fit to be classed with the most dangerous adventuresses in Europe. After this, the orthodox literary historian turns to his Poetic Encyclopaedia to find the poet who best fits with his major protagonists. Watson, I have told you often that when all else fails, the impossible must supply the truth. I propose to unlock the riddle of the sonnets by pursuing them from the impossible vantage point of the Rival Poet. I shall search out every piece of correspondence and every dedication of poems to a young patron between 1587 and 1607. Sooner or later I *must* discover the work that the Rival dedicated to the Fair Youth, and then all the threads will be in my hand.

'Come, Watson, let us go to bed. I must be off to the British Museum first thing tomorrow morning, and I may be there for many happy years.'

SONNETS.

Or layd great bafes for eternity,
Which proues more fhort then waft or ruining?
Haue I not feene dwellers on forme and fauor
Lofe all, and more by paying too much rent
For compound fweet; Forgoing fimple fauor,
Pittifull thriuors in their gazing fpent.
Noe, let me be obfequious in thy heart,
And take thou my oblacion, poore but free,
Which is not mixt with feconds, knows no art,
But mutuall render, onely me for thee.
  Hence, thou fubbornd *Informer*, a trew foule
  When moft impeacht, ftands leaft in thy controule.

126

O Thou my louely Boy who in thy power,
  Docft hould times fickle glaffe, his fickle, hower:
Who haft by wayning growne, and therein fhou'ft,
Thy louers withering, as thy fweet felfe grow'ft.
If Nature (foueraine mifteres ouer wrack)
As thou goeft onwards ftill will plucke thee backe,
She keepes thee to this purpofe, that her skill.
May time difgrace, and wretched mynuit kill.
Yet feare her O thou minnion of her pleafure,
She may detaine, but not ftill keepe her trefure!
Her *Audite* (though delayd) anfwer'd muft be,
And her *Quietus* is to render thee.
    (   )
    (   )

127

IN the ould age blacke was not counted faire,
  Or if it weare it bore not beauties name:
But now is blacke beauties fucceffiue heire,
And Beautie flanderd with a baftard fhame,
For fince each hand hath put on Natures power,
Fairing the foule with Arts faulfe borrow'd face,
Sweet beauty hath no name no holy boure,
But is prophan'd, if not liues in difgrace.

H 3   Therefore

The page in the Sonnets showing the break between 126 and 127.

65

The Lord Chamberlain's Men

WHATEVER unhappiness and humiliation Shakespeare may have been suffering in his private life, his public career was settled and assured in 1594. In that year the Earl of Derby (the former Ferdinando Lord Strange) died, and his players had to find a new patron.

They were taken under the wing of the Lord Chamberlain, Henry Carey, first Baron Hunsdon, and for the remainder of the reign the Lord Chamberlain's Men and the Admiral's Men were to be the two leading companies in the country. (For a brief period in 1596, after Hunsdon's death, while Henry Brooke, Lord Cobham served as Lord Chamberlain, they were known as Lord Hunsdon's Men after their new patron, the son of the first baron. But he succeeded to his father's office within a year, and they were again known as the Lord Chamberlain's Men.)

The original members of the company were Will Kemp, Thomas Pope, John Hemmings, Augustine Phillips and George Bryan. Within a year they had admitted Richard Burbage and William Shakespeare to their number, and for the remainder of his career, these men and their successors were Shakespeare's 'fellows'.

They were predominantly comedians at their inception. Short, fat Will Kemp was their moving spirit. Kemp's *forte* was the jig, a lively dance accompanied by a comic song with which performances concluded. By the time Shakespeare wrote *Hamlet* he seems to have been weary of some of Kemp's professional traits, and he curtly dismissed this particular skill as appealing only to 'tedious old fools' like Polonius: 'He's for a jig, or a tale of bawdry, or he sleeps.'

A satirical show at Cambridge gave some idea of the university men's view of Kemp and his style. 'Clowns have been thrust into plays by head and shoulders ever since Kemp could make a scurvy face,' remarks a character who drags a clown onto the stage by a rope. And he proceeds to describe a Kemp-like performance which would delight the groundlings:

> Why, if thou canst but draw thy mouth awry, lay thy leg over thy staff, saw a piece of cheese asunder with thy dagger, lap up drink on the earth, I warrant thee they'll laugh mightily.

Kemp was a clown in the early stage of that word's movement toward its modern meaning. Originally simply a rustic fellow or labouring countryman, the clown began by startling and amusing sophisticated audiences with his naivety and lack of urbanity.

Kemp, however, was taking low comedy a stage further. He was no mere Hodge to sit on Gammer Gurton's needle and leave it at that. When he played the part of a foolish, simple fellow, he added some personal characterisation. Thus Dogberry in *Much Ado About Nothing* was one of his roles, and while Dogberry has all the ignorance, clumsiness and malapropism traditionally ascribed to rustic clowns, he is in fact a city man; he is, moreover, distinguished by his bustling and incompetent self-importance as a constable. Kemp was noted for his skill in playing comic local dignitaries–mayors and magistrates and headboroughs. It is a pleasant thought that Shakespeare joined a company headed by the first of the long line of comic, fat policemen on the English stage.

The difficulty with Kemp, from a writer's point of view, was that his roles could not easily be integrated in plays owing their narrative structure to the conventions of Italianate romance. Too often Kemp was likely to be reduced to comic solos of stand-up patter such as we have seen in *The Two Gentlemen of Verona* and meet again in Launcelot Gobbo's part in *The Merchant of Venice*. These moments might not seem sufficiently long for an audience of apprentices and tradesmen's wives, enjoying their belly-laughs, and they might not seem sufficiently important to an actor of Kemp's standing. When we find him playing Peter in *Romeo and Juliet*–a part so

66

Henry Carey, *1st Baron Hunsdon, Lord Chamberlain.
Three years after this portrait was taken he became
patron of the company of actors Shakespeare joined. He
was first cousin to Queen Elizabeth, his mother being
Anne Boleyn's sister.*

Sir George Carey, *son of Lord Hunsdon. On his father's
death he became 2nd Baron Hunsdon, and took over the
patronage of his father's players. Within a year he, too,
became Lord Chamberlain, and the actors were again the
Chamberlain's Men.*

insignificant as to be cut from nearly all modern productions – we can hardly imagine a more wasteful use of so skilled and experienced an entertainer.

Kemp's response to his and his fans' wishes may well have been to ad lib and upstage other actors. Hamlet clearly cares about teamwork, and it has been thought that Shakespeare may have been pointing the finger at some of Kemp's mannerisms when Hamlet objects to the unartistic individualism of some clowns:

> . . . and let those that play your clowns speak
> no more than is set down for them, for there be
> of them that will themselves laugh, to set on
> some quantity of barren spectators to laugh
> too, though in the meantime some necessary
> question of the play be then to be considered.
> That's villainous and shows a most pitiful
> ambition in the fool that uses it.

If this does indeed represent Shakespeare's view of Kemp, then the role in which Kemp was best fitted into one of his plays was almost self-parody. Nick Bottom, the acting weaver of *A Midsummer Night's Dream* must have been Kemp's most interesting part, and Bottom's insistence on forcing himself into the lead role and his general sense of himself as indispensable may have represented characteristics of Kemp that the more reserved Shakespeare found intolerable.

Next in importance to Kemp was Thomas Pope, another clown. A stanza written in 1600 suggests that his clowning stuck firmly in the 'local yokel' tradition:

> Are Plough-men simple fellows nowadays?
> Not so, my Masters. What means . . .
> . . . *Pope*, the Clown, to speak so Boorish, when
> They counterfeit the Clowns upon the stage?

But Pope was not exclusively the boor. In *The Seven Deadly Sins* he played a gruff and manly general who overthrows a decadent king. A combination of the two types had led to the suggestion that Pope was the company's original *miles gloriosus*, creating roles from the fatuous Spaniard Armado in *Love's Labour's Lost* to the major role of Falstaff. But there are other claimants for Falstaff, as we shall see.

It is likely enough that Pope was at least burly, if not fat. And his home life was unusual: he never married, but took a housekeeper with the happy name of Goodwife Willingson. He trained two apprentices, Robert Gough and John Edmans. And he seems to have adopted children somewhat compulsively. He reared one Susan Gasquine from infancy; took on another girl, Mary Clark, and at the time of his death was looking after an eleven-month-old baby boy whose mother was still alive. Ben Jonson may have thought all this looked rather equivocal. In *The Poetaster*, a topical satire on the theatre, he described one fat player as a 'mango', this being a slang term for a procurer of children.

John Hemmings was a more normally domesticated

Mr. WILLIAM
SHAKESPEARES
COMEDIES,
HISTORIES, &
TRAGEDIES.

Published according to the True Originall Copies.

Martin Droeshout sculpsit London.

IONDON
Printed by Isaac Iaggard, and Ed. Blount. 1623

*William Shakespeare as a young man: Martin
Droeshout's famous engraving for the frontispiece of the
First Folio. The artist altered several details while the
book was in the press: heightening the points of light in
the eyes, untidying the hairline, and increasing the cross-
hatching. But the main features were unchanged, and at-
tested by Ben Jonson as accurate. Droeshout's engraving,
appearing eight years after Shakespeare's death, must
have followed another artist's original portrait.*

68

figure. In 1588 he married the widow of actor William Knell – the Queen's Man who was stabbed at Thame the previous year – and proceeded to beget a family of at least twelve (and possibly fifteen) children. He lived in the parish of St Mary Aldermanbury to the west of the city, and busied himself with church affairs. He was a good businessman, and it was largely his financial managerial skills after 1600 which made the Chamberlain's Men prosperous.

It is not easy to identify the roles Hemmings played. One eighteenth-century scholar claimed to have seen an Elizabethan pamphlet identifying him as Falstaff. No one else has seen such a tract, and the identification is not generally accepted today. A pamphlet that has survived calls him a tragedian. And a satirist in 1613 called him 'old stuttering Hemmings'. On this rather slender evidence he has been tentatively identified as the creator of Polonius and the line of more or less benevolent, fussy older men from Boyet in *Love's Labour's Lost* to Gonzalo in *The Tempest*.

Augustine Phillips lived near Kemp and Pope in the parish of St Saviour's on the Bankside. Henslowe and Alleyn both lived there, too, conveniently near the Rose, and they both became vestrymen. Phillips and his wife brought up five children in the parish. There may have been some unpleasant gossip about them: a letter to Henslowe signed 'A.P.' asks him to disregard any scandal he hears about the writer's wife, and Anne Phillips remarried most unsuitably after her husband's death. This suggestive evidence, together with the fact that Augustine played the role of the effeminate Sardinapolus in *The Seven Deadly Sins* has led to the speculation that Phillips may have played gallant and personable, but slightly sinister, roles culminating in Claudius.

But as a professional colleague Phillips was clearly up to the high standard generally represented by the Chamberlain's Men. By the end of the decade he was stage managing or generally arranging their productions. At his death he left his heirs such a collection of musical instruments that it has been suggested that he may have been more important to the company as a musician than as an actor.

George Bryan lived just across the river in Blackfriars. He had travelled in Denmark with Kemp and Pope during a tour made by Leicester's Men in the 1580s, when the English players had been very well received at Elsinore. He seems to have been a 'straight man', distinguished by his 'able body and goodly shape'.

Shakespeare and Burbage were working with these men before their admission to formal company membership. Burbage had been in the 1590 production of *The Seven Deadly Sins*. Shakespeare's *Titus Andronicus* was performed by Derby's Men, Pembroke's Men and Sussex's Men which suggests that its author's allegiances were unsettled before 1594. Shakespeare's residence at

Shakespeare's fellow actor William Sly. A former apprentice of Augustine Phillips, he was made a full member soon after Shakespeare and Burbage.

this time was perfectly sited for access to the older theatres. He lodged at Bishopsgate Street in St Helen's parish, halfway between the Shoreditch theatres and the Gracechurch Street innyards. Burbage lived near his family's theatre in Shoreditch.

Richard Burbage was a talented man. A painter as well as an actor, the portrait of him that survives is from his own hand. When Shakespeare's characters describe their plays' heroes, they often refer to the chestnut curls visible in Burbage's self-portrait, faded though they had grown in his maturity. The Burbage of the 1590s was also clean-shaven, unlike the Burbage of the portrait: many references are made to the slim beardlessness of such roles of his as Prince Hal.

Shakespeare was not clean shaven. One of the two definite portraits of him we have is the engraving by Martin Droeshout serving as frontispiece to the First Folio edition of his plays. Though it is a stiff and unrealistic piece of work, probably copied from a painting (Droeshout being too young to have known Shakespeare at the age at which he is depicted) a verse by Ben Jonson nonetheless commends it as a good likeness.

It shows that Shakespeare in his twenties had grown a light moustache which he combed upward, and a tuft of hair beneath his lower lip. His most striking feature was his high, domed forehead, accentuated by prematurely receding hair. What hair remained was combed in loose waves over his ears. His lower lip was full; the upper clearly bowed. Fine eyebrows traced a clearly marked ridge of bone, and his large, clear eyes were set over marked pouches. His nose was well shaped, and only the excessive length given the face by the high forehead robbed it of a handsome appearance.

Possibly the ageing dignity of this premature baldness led to his taking kingly roles. At any rate, an epigram by John Davies of Hereford makes great play with Shakespeare's having 'played some kingly parts' and thus having 'a reigning wit'. We notice that the kings and dukes of Shakespeare's own plays, though rarely the true central characters, tend always to be given a moment or moments in which their social seniority really counts, and they appear to dominate the stage from the centre. These parts seem more like the creations of a reasonably modest actor writing with himself in mind than does the limiting character role of Adam in *As You Like It*, which is the part played by Shakespeare according to the most plausible tradition to come down to us. The tradition that he played the ghost in *Hamlet* does not conflict with the ascription of kingly roles to Shakespeare: Claudius is more villain than ruler in that story, and the ghost is the embodiment of the highest social standing in the Elsinore of the play.

Most of the actors had apprentices. Acting was not a recognised craft bound by Guild statutes and practices. But the custom of the time clearly influenced the actors, and they took boy performers into their homes, made themselves responsible for their professional training, and remembered them in their wills. Henry Condell and William Sly were the next two full members inducted into the company after Shakespeare and Burbage: they seem to have been apprenticed to Hemmings and Phillips respectively. Burbage seems to have looked after young Nick Tooley. Kemp may have been William Eccleston's master. Shakespeare, living alone in lodgings with no apprentice, was decidedly the odd man out among his fecundly domestic fellows.

Hired men were necessary to fill out the numbers of roles in full-scale Elizabethan drama. They might be described as the company's musicians or attendants, and swelled a crowd when they were not delivering a few lines.

The names of some of them have come down to us, accidentally embedded in the printed texts of plays where the printer, following a manuscript lent by the theatre, copied the stage manager's note where he had scribbled in the name of the particular extra he had to call instead of his character-name. William Toyer carried a trumpet in *A Midsummer Night's Dream*. Jack Wilson was a singing boy. He played Balthazar in *Much Ado About Nothing*; never apparently graduated to adult acting status; and may have stayed principally as a musician all his life. Hired men called Harvey and Russel took part in *Henry VI*, and nearly ten years later, Russel was still with the company to create the role of Bardolph. One striking hired man was John Sinklo or Sinckler (Sinclair?) whose gaunt appearance won him such identifiable minor roles as the legitimate Falconbridge in *King John* and the Apothecary in *Romeo and Juliet*.

This then was the established company. It would change its name once more, and replenish itself with new members as old ones died or disappeared. But it would never itself disband or cease business until the Puritans closed all theatres fifty years later. It was to establish a new and inimitable model of co-operative theatre company management; to pioneer new and higher standards of drama; and to secure the prosperity of all its members.

Membership of a leading company of players was an excellent position for Shakespeare the writer. Not only did he have an immediate market for his scripts, he also had the financial security of a means of livelihood that did not depend on the freshness of his creative imagination. And he enjoyed the unusual advantage of profiting by the success of his own work. Most playwrights sold their scripts to the actors, and then, like Greene, watched with indignant frustration if they had received a bad bargain and the actors made a vast commercial profit out of the words which they now owned. Shakespeare was buyer rather than seller of his writing, and shared in the profits.

The Chamberlain's Men were lucky not to be dominated as were the Admiral's Men by a financially unscrupulous backer petting his starring relative. Nobody who wrote for Henslowe after 1594 had any reason to be grateful to the old man, who treated his writers even worse than he treated actors (apart from Ned Alleyn). Henslowe, indeed, would have consorted very well with the Hollywood moguls of the 1930s and '40s. He kept his actors on tight contracts; treated his writers as the merest hacks; and practised shameless nepotism.

Nor was Shakespeare under the influence of an aristocratic patron and his demoralising clique of hangers-on. He was one of a confident group of hard-working men who had risen to the top by their own skill and industry. They called on his creative gifts for practical ends, though as one of the inner circle he may have enjoyed seeing that his work was not tampered with, and he seems to have taken little part in the collaborative writing so prominent in plays of the 1590s. Once, though, he may have let himself be called in as a script doctor.

Shakespeare at Work

HENRY CHETTLE, hot from the writing of *Kind Heart's Dream*, proceeded to turn playwright. Before his death in 1607, he had written thirteen plays (of which only one survives) and collaborated on thirty-six others (of which four survive). At some time in the 1590s, he joined a group of collaborators who were trying to patch up a play Anthony Munday had written about Sir Thomas More.

The patching was not needed because the play was badly written; Munday was a competent hack whose forte was plotting, and anyway, the voracious late Elizabethan theatre never allowed mere bad writing to prevent performance. The problem was political.

The government evidently feared that certain scenes in the play would arouse England's traditional anti-immigrant feeling. In his early days, More, as Sheriff of London had put down the rioting which broke out on 'Ill May-Day' against Lombard immigrants. It may be that Munday wished to cash in on the topicality of this theme, now that there was much feeling against the Huguenot immigrants: at any rate, nearly a quarter of his play dealt with the incident and its repercussions.

Munday was the last man to ignore political pressure to revise. Ten years older than Shakespeare, his career had been more sinister than Marlowe's. As a young man he had travelled to Rome and masqueraded as a Catholic sympathiser, using the information he obtained from hospitable English Catholics there as the basis of anti-Catholic pamphlets when he returned home. For a short time he worked for the odious Richard Topcliffe, a private witch-hunter who was licensed by the government to ferret out Catholic priests – and who enjoyed the right to interrogate and torture suspects in his own house. Munday brought unusual notoriety even to Topcliffe's gang of spies and informers: he was detected by Walsingham's men in robbing a widow as he purported to search her property for Papist objects of devotion.

After 1584 he concentrated upon writing for the theatre, and became one of the most prominent figures in the world of public entertainment. He obtained control of the London City Pageants from 1600 onwards, and retained a vast collection of costumes and properties that he leased to any other writers who produced spectacles for the burghers. Anthony Munday knew, from the inside, how remorseless were the workings of Tudor government inquisition. If a play of his needed political revision, it should have it.

In addition to Chettle, four other people contributed their ideas and passages in their handwriting, to the still extant manuscript *The Book of Sir Thomas More*. (Already in theatrical jargon, a working script was called 'the book of the play'.) One was a professional scribe, two others were apparently playwrights succeeding in the new mode of bourgeois drama. Thomas Heywood claimed to have 'had either an entire hand or at least a main finger' in no less than 220 plays, and in explaining the non-publication of the majority of them, he lifts the veil over the working conditions from which Shakespeare's plays were providentially saved for us by his loyal colleagues. 'Many of them,' Heywood noted, 'by shifting and change of the companies have been negligently lost.'

Thomas Dekker, likewise, had a hand in a great many plays, having a well deserved reputation as a 'dresser' of old scripts. He was an excellent hack writer who never succeeded, like Anthony Munday, in finding himself a secure financial base. Within a month of starting to write under contract to Henslowe, Dekker was within need of a loan to rescue himself from debtors' prison.

Some shifting and change of the companies must have thrown these Admiral's Men into collaboration with Shakespeare, for Heywood, too, worked for Henslowe, tied by an iniquitous contract which demonstrates clearly how lucky the Chamberlain's Men were to be dependent on no such 'angel'.

A page from The Book of Sir Thomas More *which many scholars believe to be Shakespeare's autograph. The heavy crossing out a third of the way down the page is not Shakespeare's, but the work of a scrivener, who substituted the inserted words, 'Tell me but this'.*

Memorandum that this 25 March 1598 Thomas Heywood came and hired himself with me as a covenant servant for 2 years by the receiving of 2 single pence according to the Statute of Winchester & to begin at the day above written & not to play anywhere public about London not while these 2 years be expired but in my house if he do then he doth forfeit unto me by the receiving of these 2d. forty pounds.

Shakespeare seems to have helped these employee-victims of Henslowe's, for the fourth hand to appear on the manuscript has been tentatively identified as his.

There are three major grounds on which the identification is proposed. One is the handwriting. Handwriting experts concur that the passages of *Sir Thomas More* written in the hand known as D could have been written by Shakespeare. They base this conclusion on a comparison with his known signatures on legal documents, and the additional words 'by me' before the signature on his will. For many, this is an insufficient sample for the comparison to be taken to any further conclusion. But some feel that there are sufficient unique features in the Shakespeare signatures to justify the assertion of a definite identity between his hand and Hand D. They draw attention in particular to a peculiar 'spurred' a.

The second ground for claiming that Hand D is Shakespeare's lies in the spelling. Some peculiar orthographical features of the early printed texts of the plays have long led scholars to believe that the printers must at times have been working from author's manuscripts, and reproducing some of his spelling mannerisms. It seems, for instance, that Shakespeare usually spelled 'one' as 'on'. He used the form 'a leven' for 'eleven'. And he produced the unique form 'scilens' for 'silence'. These, and numerous other characteristics believed to be Shakespearean are found in Hand D's passages of *Sir Thomas More*.

Finally, the content and style of Hand D's contribution seems entirely Shakespearean. His major passage is the important scene in which the anti-immigrant riot is checked by More. It is generally agreed that the handling of the mob in this scene is thoroughly consonant with Shakespeare's usual treatment of crowd scenes. The rioters are used effectively for comic purposes. They are good-natured, but ignorant and not very sharp. They are fickle and are visibly swayed by oratory. All this

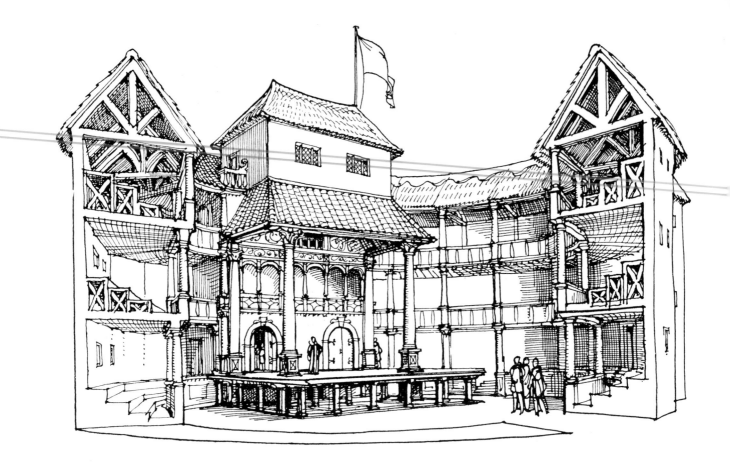

they have in common with Shakespearean mobs in *Henry VI*, *Julius Caesar* and *Coriolanus*.

More's speech to the mob reveals further Shakespearean attitudes. He argues that the rioters themselves must ultimately desire stability, and cannot therefore wish to win their case by establishing a precedent for popular violence. This accords generally with the impression of philosophic conservatism made by most of Shakespeare's work. But More's development of the argument is more precisely Shakespearean. To oppose lawful authority is, he says, to oppose God. Kings are lent their authority by God and are godlike on earth. A King is owed obedience, without which the state will fall apart, as the rioters must see by perceiving that the effectiveness of their own uprising depends entirely on their obedience to their leaders. Yet those leaders being themselves rebels against authority, how can they expect to exact obedience in the future when their own example tells against them?

Here we have a definite sequence of thought that we may assume Shakespeare would certainly have recognised and probably have endorsed. It is expounded in Ulysses' long speech on 'degree' (or rank) in *Troilus and Cressida*: it is supported by the recurrent images of the state as one body in *Coriolanus*: and the problems suggested by the speech are at the root of the dramatic tension of his second tetralogy of history plays.

But if Shakespeare did lend a hand to help the play past the censors with a strongly loyalist exposition of

A playhouse, c. 1595 realised by C. Walter Hodges and based on Johannes de Witt's sketch. By permission of the author and the Oxford University Press, from The Globe Restored.

subjects' duties, his efforts were in vain. The Master of the Revels sent the script back with an uncompromising rejection:

> Leave out the insurrection wholly & the Cause thereof & begin with Sir Tho. Moore at the mayor's sessions with A report of his good service done being Sheriff of London upon a mutiny Against the Lombards only by A short report and not otherwise at your own perils
>
> E. Tilney

The play was never performed.

The importance of the probably Shakespearean fragment is that it seems to offer us a sample of his work as he was in the process of composition: that it takes us directly into his workroom, and permits us to compare a passage written in his own hand with the reports of his methods left by contemporaries.

There are two such reports of some importance. The first comes from his two fellows, Hemmings and Condell, in their 'Letter to the Great Variety of Readers' prefixed to the First Folio. They report that

> His mind and hand went together: And what he thought he uttered with that easiness, that we have scarce received from him a blot in his papers.

He was, in other words, a fluent and rapid writer, whose first thoughts were so satisfactory that he had to make very few revisions and alterations.

The second contemporary witness commented on this view, and agreed that it represented Shakespeare's practice, though he was not willing to see it as praiseworthy. In *Timber: or, Discoveries; Made upon Men and Matter*, a grandiloquently titled selection from his notebooks, Ben Jonson observed

> I *remember*, the Players have often mentioned it as an honour to *Shakespeare*, that in his writing, (whatsoever he penn'd) he never blotted out a line. My answer hath been, would he had blotted a thousand. Which they thought a malevolent speech. I had not told posterity this, but for their ignorance, who choose that circumstance to commend their friend by, wherein he most faulted.

Jonson went on to explain why he thought this rapid execution a weakness. Shakespeare

> had an excellent *Fantasy* [imagination]; brave notions [bold ideas] and gentle expressions [elegant phrasing]: wherein he flow'd with that facility, that sometimes it was necessary he should be stopp'd. . . . Many times he fell into those things, could not escape laughter: As when he said in the person of *Caesar*, one speaking to him; *Caesar* thou dost me wrong. He replied: *Caesar did never wrong, but with just cause* and such like: which were ridiculous.

Shakespeare, in Jonson's view, composed too fast, and so slipped into making Irish bulls. Apparently he persuaded Shakespeare that this might be the case, for the example he cites is no longer to be found in *Julius Caesar*. In its place is the more syntactically rational, less metrically accurate line and a half,

> Know Caesar doth not wrong, nor without
> Will he be satisfied.   cause

Jonson's opinion did not change. Towards the end of his life he walked to Scotland, and while there passed a drunken, gossippy evening with the minor poet, William Drummond. He told Drummond that

> Shakespeare wanted art . . . Shakespeare, in a play brought in a number of men saying they had suffered Shipwreck in Bohemia, where there is no Sea near by some 100 miles.

How, then, do the Hand D additions to the *Sir Thomas More* manuscript support this view of a startlingly facile composer? Very well, in fact. There are no lengthy corrections. The only place at which more than one word is erased comes at a difficult passage which clearly passed the professional scribe's comprehension. He, therefore, and not Shakespeare, struck out four lines, and substituted in their place the naive linking phrase, 'Tell me but this.' In a passage of 140 lines, Shakespeare made

only eighteen alterations, and in every case he simply struck out one word or part of an uncompleted word, and raced on with his instant substitution.

He was keen on employing abbreviations, and so could produce mysterious words like pfnyp (parsnip). When he carelessly forgot to add the squiggles by which Elizabethans demonstrated that they were using abbreviations, he could produce further mysteries, like 'matie' for 'majesty'.

A lack of that pedantic 'art' approved by Jonson is also apparent in his complete disregard for any consistent spelling. In an age where freedom of orthography was normal, Shakespeare pushed that freedom to the limit, and was not even consistent with himself. Perhaps the most striking instance of this is a line in which the crowd calls for More. There are only two words employed, 'Shrieve' (sheriff) and 'More'. Shakespeare manages to repeat a spelling only once in the entire line:

Shreiue moor moor more Shreue moore.

(He has elsewhere two more variants on shrieve: 'Sheriff' and 'shreef'.)

His punctuation is almost non-existent. At times when he does put it in, he seems to allow himself two quick shots at alternative pauses, scribbling ,: or ;⋅ – the fullstop floating midway up the line is one of his favourite marks.

Another habit suggests that he was swept along by the pace of the scene unwinding in his imagination rather than a slow fabricator of illusion. He pays little attention to speech prefixes, particularly in his crowd scene. He received a script from Munday in which the leaders of the mob were identified as John Lincoln, Williamson and his wife Doll, Sherwin, George Betts and Ralph Betts the Clown. Shakespeare, having identified his principal speaker as Lincoln (shortening steadily through 'Linco' and 'Linc' to 'Lin') was content for a while to have him exchange sallies with an unidentified 'other' (soon shortened to 'oth'). He identified Doll whenever he wanted a woman's voice from the crowd, but never bothered to distinguish between the two Bettses. It was left to the professional scribe to go back and sort out the tangle of Bettses, and identify the secondary other speakers, as he had also to check Shakespeare's vague and inaccurate listing of the entries and departures of groups of characters.

Shakespeare's creative mind, as (and of course, if) revealed by these pages, seems to be that of an impassioned participant actor or enrapt spectator. The Stage Manager's needs were the last thing he thought of. The stage spectacle, the movement, and the conflict of voices came first. If he needed a new voice to change the pace or direction of a scene, that voice was down on the page, speaking before he had reflected on where or how the character was to be brought on stage. Dreary details were for some one else. This mind was overflowing with creative life.

Theatre Problems

THE CHRISTMAS season of 1594-5 saw the newly formed Lord Chamberlain's Men professionally busy. On 26 and 27 December they performed before the Queen at Greenwich. The following March, Shakespeare, Kemp and Burbage collected the company's payment for that entertainment.

On 28 December the young gentlemen of Gray's Inn hired the players to perform 'A Comedy of Errors (like to Plautus his Menechmus)'. After Oxford and Cambridge (which took students at a younger age than is now the case) graduates proceeded to the Inns at what we should now recognise as an undergraduate age. Their Christmas festivities generally displayed the satirical wit and boisterous fun we now associate with undergraduate high spirits, and this note is sounded clearly in the cheeky record the young men wrote up of their Christmas festivities of 1594. There had been some confusion and overcrowding in the hall prior to the players' arrival, and the students solemnly blamed this on an imaginary

> Sorceror or Conjuror that was supposed to be the Cause of that confused Inconvenience . . . And . . . he had foisted a Company of base and common Fellows to make up our Disorders with a Play of Errors and Confusions; and . . . that Night had gained to us Discredit, and itself a Nickname of Errors.

A year later, the Company may have been called upon to give a private Christmas entertainment in the house of the diplomatist and courtier Sir Edward Hoby in Cannon Street. At any rate, in December he wrote to Sir Robert Cecil, inviting him to dinner, and adding that 'K. Richard [would] present him self to your view.' This is taken to be a promise of a performance of *Richard II*.

During 1596 a new theatre was built on the South Bank. This was the Swan in Paris Garden, well to the west of the Rose and its near neighbour the Bear Garden. The Chamberlain's Men may have started acting in the Swan at this time. The Burbages had by now fallen two years in arrears with their rent to the ground landlord of the theatre, and their building was twenty years old and in a poor state of repair. By contrast, a Dutch visitor who was thoroughly impressed with London's theatres, commented

> Of all the theatres, however, the finest and biggest is that whose sign is a swan (commonly called the Swan theatre), for it will seat 3,000 people, is built of a concrete of flints . . . and is supported by wooden columns so painted as to deceive the most acute observer into thinking they are marble . . . it appears to resemble a Roman building.

The entrepreneur responsible for this triumph of modernity was Francis Langley, a goldsmith who proposed to operate his new investment along the lines laid down by Henslowe: letting it to companies who should be bound to play for him, and taking half the profits.

Like other theatre proprieters, Langley had his troubles with the local authorities. The Lord Mayor of London personally attempted to persuade Burghley not to let him build the theatre in the first place. When this failed, it remained open to the local justices to harass Langley, especially during the latter part of 1596 and early 1597 when old Lord Hunsdon, the drama-loving Lord Chamberlain died, and was replaced by Henry Brooke, 7th Lord Cobham.

The importance of the Lord Chamberlain to all actors (not merely those Hunsdon had patronised) was that he could claim that their performances at court made them at least Honorary Members of the Royal Household, and therefore subject to his jurisdiction rather than that of the Puritan magistracy. Lord Cobham, proud of his descent from the Lollard Sir John Oldcastle, preferred Puritan magistrates to players, and made no attempt to protect the drama. Tom Nashe commented sympathetically on the position of Shakespeare and his fellows, who had thought themselves secure in the personal patronage of a sympathetic Lord Chamberlain: now they were

> piteously persecuted by the Lord Mayor, and
> however in their old lord's time they thought
> their state settled, it is now so uncertain they
> cannot build on it.

Inside the City, where his writ ran directly, the Lord Mayor firmly closed down the Gracechurch Street innyard playhouses, robbing the Chamberlain's Men (or Lord Hunsdon's Men as they were at this juncture) of their normal winter quarters.

James Burbage, enterprising as ever, thought he had the answer to this difficulty. The 'Liberty' of Blackfriars was a superior residential district inside the City bounds, but privileged to be free from the jurisdiction of the Lord Mayor. Here Burbage bought for £600 part of the old priory that had formerly been used by the boy players, and converted it elaborately and expensively into a first-rate indoor theatre. It was completed in November 1596, and Lord Hunsdon's Men should have been secure in the possession of the newest and most up-to-date theatre in London.

But their hopes were dashed. James Burbage had not troubled to secure the good will of the Blackfriars residents, and his carpenters had made an abominable noise in converting the theatre to his needs. The fashionable householders of the neighbourhood did not want to be jostled by crowds of citizens coming to the plays. They petitioned the Privy Council for the theatre to be stopped from mounting performances, and the new Lord Chamberlain did nothing to help the actors. So Burbage's proud new theatre lay unused, and the frustration probably hastened his death.

Still, in this case James Burbage's carelessness in preparing his ground had been monumental. The petition was headed by his own patron, the 2nd Lord Hunsdon!

Over on the South Bank, Francis Langley was having difficulty with a peculiarly unpleasant magistrate. James Gardiner was an unscrupulous miser who received a welcome directive on 22 July 1596, the day of the first Lord Hunsdon's death. An immediate order went out that plays were to be prohibited in London and the suburbs, 'For that by drawing together of much people increase of sickness is feared.' The suburbs included the Bankside. The plague was an unanswerable reason for closing the theatres. Only there is no evidence that the plague was particularly rampant at that time.

Gardiner will have had no regret in forcing temporary closure on Langley's palatial investment. In May that year Langley had called him 'a false knave; a false forsworn knave, and a perjured knave'. There was little exaggeration in these remarks, but Gardiner sued

Sir Edward Hoby, who is believed to have presented a performance of Richard II *at his house in Cannon Street in 1595.*

Langley for slander. Langley gave evidence of occasions on which Gardiner had perjured himself, and pleaded justification. Gardiner lamely objected that Langley had used the words with respect to a particular dispute between the two of them, and ought not to be allowed to defend himself by reference to other occasions of his notoriety. Then he dropped the case before it could come to trial.

But threats and abuse passed between the two men. It was not beneath Gardiner to try to get his way by intimidation, and early in November Langley swore out a writ against Gardiner and one William Wayte charging them with uttering threats and menaces. This Wayte was Gardiner's son-in-law, a feeble tool whom Gardiner had robbed and exploited and altogether made a perfect Roderigo to his own Iago.

Gardiner knew the ways of the law. The best way to protect himself against the implication of intimidation was to swear out a counter-writ charging his accuser with similar conduct, so that the courts would dismiss the whole affair as a foolish, intemperate quarrel. Wayte was pushed forward to take the prominent role in this manoeuvre, and was evidently expected to involve some of Langley's friends and supporters. So it was that in late November, 1596, William Shakespeare found himself accused before the Court of Queen's Bench of having

Sir John Oldcastle, the Lollard leader of the time of Henry V, whom Shakespeare originally intended as Prince Hal's fat companion. When Oldcastle's descendants, the Brookes, objected, Shakespeare changed the name to Falstaff.

Henry Brooke, 8th Lord Cobham, kept up his father's objection to the portrayal of his ancestor, Oldcastle, as a drunken rogue, and may have succeeded in excluding Falstaff from Henry V. *He was himself nicknamed 'Falstaff' by Essex and Southampton.*

threatened 'death and so forth' to William Wayte. Charged with him were Langley, and two women about whom nothing is known: Dorothy Soer and Anne Lee.

The case went no further. The exchange of writs was sufficient, apparently, to calm things down. But out of this we have the certainty that by November 1596 Shakespeare had left his Bishopsgate lodgings and moved to the Liberty of the Clink on Bankside, and the fact that he was an associate of Langley's (from which we may infer that the Chamberlain's Men were at least considering acting in the Swan). It is likely enough, too, that Shakespeare knew and disliked Gardiner.

The harassment of the theatres in 1596-97 left its mark in the three Falstaff plays Shakespeare was writing at the time. He originally named his fat knight 'Sir John Oldcastle'. Whether he deliberately set out to offend Oldcastle's descendant, Lord Cobham, cannot be definitely decided, but offence was certainly taken, and the name had to be changed to Falstaff. Even after the chilly Lord Chamberlain's death his son maintained a threatening attitude to theatrical mockery of his ancestor. The actors were forced to put a mealy-mouthed apology into the epilogue of *Henry IV part 2*:

> our humble author will continue the story,
> with Sir John in it . . . where, for anything I
> know, Falstaff shall die of a sweat, unless 'a be
> killed with your hard opinions; for Oldcastle
> died a martyr, and this is not the man.

It may have been Cobham's hard opinions that caused Falstaff to die prematurely.

Cobham, too, was likely enough to be the target of jealous Master Ford's disguising himself as *Brooke* in *The Merry Wives of Windsor*. Brooke was the family name of the Cobhams, and once again Shakespeare was forced to make a change, by making Brooke into Broome. This, of course, lost a good deal of the punning fun about Fords and Brookes.

The Merry Wives of Windsor exploited the great comic crew devised for the *Henry IV* plays to offer entertainment at the installation of Knights of the Garter in April 1597, when the Company's patron, George Lord Hunsdon was installed, as was the Duke of Würtemburg, Elizabeth's 'Cousin Mumpellgart'. The latter was so notorious a bore that he was quietly given the knighthood he desired in absentia, and Elizabeth never did get round to sending him the insignia. Würtemburg's absence seems to be glanced at in the play's chaff about the Host's horses, stolen by missing 'cousins-german' and 'garmombles'.

It has been further proposed that Justice Gardiner is attacked in this play. He had married a Lucy, and quartered their arms with his own, so that the 'dozen white luces' of Shallow's coat-of-arms might point to him rather than to Sir Thomas of Charlcote.

Tradition has asserted, since the early eighteenth century, that Elizabeth herself commissioned *The Merry*

*The Swan Theatre, dominating the surrounding houses
on Bankside.*

*Below : Elizabethan Windsor, where the formal
ceremonies of the Order of the Garter were held.
Search Windsor Castle, elves, within and out . . .
The several chains of order look you scour . . .
And nightly, meadow-fairies, look you sing
Like to the Garter's compass, in a ring*
    The Merry Wives of Windsor. *V, V, 56-66.*

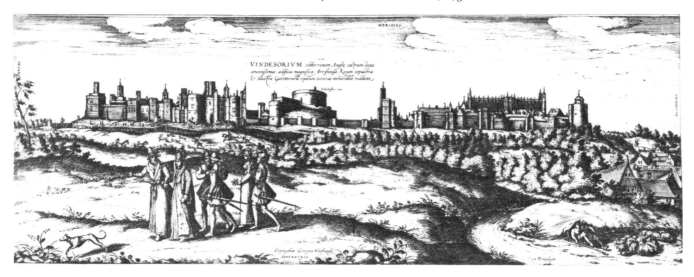

Wives of Windsor, saying that she wished to see 'the knight in love'. It is a fact that the first printed edition of the play stated clearly that it had been performed before the Queen. It is highly probable that this performance took place in Westminster on St George's Day, one month before the newly elected knights were to proceed to Windsor for their installation proper. Elizabeth did not accompany them there, and Shakespeare's 'Fairy Queen' directs the 'Fairies' to decorate and furbish Windsor without herself going with them. One must agree with general critical opinion that, charming though the play as a whole is, Falstaff is a pale shadow of the great character of the histories.

Ben Jonson (1572–1637) by an unknown artist. A steadfast friend and admirer of Will Shakespeare, who persuaded his company, the Lord Chamberlain's Men, to present Ben Jonson's plays.

Petition of the residents of the Liberty of Blackfriars against James Burbage's right to open his new indoor theatre in 1596.

The difficulties the actors experienced with Cobham may have hastened the retirement of George Bryan. At any rate, around this time he left the company, and his place was filled by Richard Cowley, a comedian who played Verges to Kemp's Dogberry, and may have specialised in thin, silly old men.

The Swan remained an unlucky theatre. After Cobham's death Pembroke's Men moved into the Swan. Before 1597 was out they mounted Tom Nashe's play *The Isle of Dogs*. This satire so appalled the government that it closed *all* the theatres, issued directions (never carried out) to the Bankside magistrates to rip out the stage and galleries from the Swan, and was loth to allow acting to recommence in Langley's theatre even after they had let Henslowe reopen the Rose. When Langley did reopen his splendid theatre, he was unable to maintain a steady succession of plays, and gradually the Swan declined to a centre of varying sorts of spectacle, but little legitimate drama.

It was at this juncture that Shakespeare's most successful professional rival emerged in the theatre. Ben Jonson began to act (far less successfully than Shakespeare) with Pembroke's Men, and was imprisoned with them for his part in *The Isle of Dogs*. On his release he began to write plays for several of the existing companies. *Every Man In His Humour* and *Every Man Out of His Humour* were performed by the Lord Chamberlain's Men, and according to eighteenth-century tradition it was Shakespeare who persuaded his fellows to accept them.

Jonson was a robust and vigorous man. In 1598 he fought with and killed Gabriel Spencer, an actor who had once been a hired man with Lord Strange's Men, and who had been imprisoned with him after *The Isle of Dogs*. Jonson escaped punishment by pleading benefit of clergy, that obsolete law that allowed the literate one first offence unpunished on the grounds that, being able to read a verse from the Bible, they must be clerics entitled to trial by the ecclesiastical and not the civil courts.

Abruptly he turned Catholic: equally abruptly, twelve years later, he reverted to Protestantism.

He blithely attacked other writers – notably, in the satirical play *The Poetaster*, John Marston. This led to the so-called 'War of the Theatres' in which Jonson and others exchanged obscure satirical abuse through their plays for a few years. He was far touchier about his standing as a writer than Shakespeare, and was the first playwright to value his work so highly as to bring out a volume of his own collected plays.

To most contemporaries, Jonson seemed a greater writer than Shakespeare. His comparatively frigid tragedies were more firmly rooted in classical models than any of his contemporaries, and his poetry was immensely successful in retaining grace and elegance, while replacing the sugary ornament of earlier Elizabethan lyrics with classical directness and simplicity. He had a talent that Shakespeare certainly could not match for creating robust, forceful, farcical situation comedy. What he lacked was Shakespeare's hint of melancholy beneath the surface of comedy, and the limpid beauty of his verse, which combine to give an ethereal quality to the romantic comedies.

Jonson's characters are closer to caricature than Shakespeare's, and he had none of Shakespeare's interest in creating charming groups of witty young aristocrats. Good farce, powered by the mainsprings of lust and avarice, was to prove Jonson's forte. Idyllic comedy, revolving around love and misunderstanding was Shakespeare's preference.

Jonson was a firm friend of Shakespeare's. 'I loved the man this side idolatry' he declared. But his competitive, combative nature kept him persistently critical of what he saw as weaknesses in his friend's work; only once, in commemorative and commendatory verses attached to the First Folio, paying an utterly magnanimous, spontaneous tribute to the truly magnificent qualities he saw in his work. I don't suppose Jonson ever doubted that his own work was superior to Shakespeare's, and it is quite probable that the less assertive Shakespeare shared this common opinion. But if Shakespeare was unjustly shouldered aside by Jonson in their own day, it is Jonson who must now be seen as unfortunate in having Shakespeare as a contemporary. A fine writer, who dominated his age, he is now severely under-regarded because of his inferiority to his friend.

A country wedding, 1590. About a mile south of the river, opposite the Tower of London, this village gives an impression of the sort of place Newington Butts was when the third English theatre opened there. Where the village stood is now the great junction of London streets called the Elephant and Castle.

Histories and Comedies

AFTER THE prentice period and the poems, Shakespeare's work to the end of the century was dominated by his second tetralogy of history plays and his comedies. True, there was *Romeo and Juliet* which showed that his capacity to write tragedy was not fairly indicated by *Titus Andronicus*.

It is a tragedy of pathos and prettiness. No profound moral truths are uncovered in the course of the play, and no characters of heroic stature emerge. Nor is the nature of love explored very deeply or widely. The audience may almost fill in for itself the young people's thrill of love at first sight, and then weep for the poor young things: it is a play whose tragic element, indeed, seems to resolve itself into just such cliches. The comic elements – the wit of Mercutio and the bawdry of the Nurse – seem much more surely created.

The second cycle of histories, on the other hand, contains one of Shakespeare's greatest and most lasting creations – Falstaff! There were many traditions (apparently quite well founded) that Henry V had been something of a wild young man and reformed suddenly on acceding to the throne. These stories justified the creation of a central, exemplary, dissolute companion, who could be used to show the effects of political events in many curious walks of life.

At his best, Falstaff is the genius of comedy in a state of drunken fatigue. Always the perfect companion for an evening's drinking and whoring, he shows us both the pleasure of his company and the danger it entails in the brilliant tavern scene in Part 2. The pleasure lies in the slackly casual, unbuttoned acceptance of the immediate and coarse pleasures of life. If the huge man with the

benevolent white beard enjoys guzzling his sack and fondling his whore, why shouldn't we do the same? It hasn't brought him to an early grave, or penury, or friendlessness, or any of the other states that Puritanism is always threatening us with if we enjoy ourselves. True, he complains of the pox, but he turns that into a joke, so it can't be so dreadful, after all. He is everyone's ideal boon companion and drinking crony. Shakespeare may have pleaded sickness to avoid roistering himself, but he thoroughly understood its appeal to others.

But he knew, too, the danger. Falstaff's companionship with the prince is bought at the expense of his dignity. He must let himself be insulted as the mood takes his royal companion. He has no means of recovery but counter-insult, and he must swallow that and turn it to flattery if challenged. And what with his lies, his flattery, his abuse, his mock-humility, none of it deeply felt, words have ceased to have real meaning for him. Falstaff's life is one of fuddled delusion. What he thinks important is unimportant, and he puts no value on things that really do matter. Those he calls his friends will cheat him or drop him at a moment's notice. He can buy a night of Doll Tearsheet's company, but cannot command a moment of her respect. Like the prince and Poins, the hard-headed whore sees him as ridiculously old to be playing the young rip. And she only melts toward him in moments when the fuddling combination of drink and sentimentality have wrecked her own sense of reality.

When Doll's realism does assert itself, she reminds Falstaff of the one word he fears and whose meaning he cannot escape. Death. We may like Falstaff for his apparent enjoyment of life. But Shakespeare warns us that this hectic carousing may be a negative aspect of that love: the terror of death.

And within two scenes, Shakespeare whisks us from his wonderful, profound, funny, utterly realistic tavern of the city to the equally English, equally realistic, equally Falstaffian scene at Justice Shallow's in the country. Shakespeare never ceased to be a countryman. His appreciation of English scenery was striking: in an age when an artificial and enamelled use of floral imagery was mandatory in poetry, he is forever startling us with his realistic, non-conventional observation of fields and flowers and animals. His imagery carries a persistently rural flavour: in this Gloucestershire scene, the thorough townsman Falstaff sweeps us momentarily to a Warwickshire river bank, as he plots to cheat Shallow with the words, 'If the young dace be a bait for the old pike, I see no reason in the law of nature but I may snap at him.'

Yet Shakespeare is totally unsentimental in his creation of country life. He knows the existence is peaceful and placid: money can be made from selling a few bullocks, and keeping an eye on the value of land, and deciding what to plant a field with next year. But it all seems a little tame. The great aim of the country boy is to get to town and see some life as soon as possible. The memories of the old countryman dwell on the great things he has done outside the rural idyll in which he lives. And so old Shallow sits and lies and boasts about his student days, and the more he claims to have been a

The South Bank shortly after Shakespeare's death. Loggan clearly worked from older maps rather than direct sketches: his Globe (36) looks more like the old than the new building, and he has not attended to Henslowe's renaming of the Bear Garden (37) as the Hope. The huts shown on it may, however, represent part of Henslowe's remodelling. The comparative isolation of the Swan in Paris Garden (38) is well brought out.

N as before the Fire

sophisticated young urbanite, the more he proves to Falstaff and us that he is a simple old bucolic.

He proves, too, the attractions of Falstaff and all he represents. In real terms, Shallow is a more prosperous man than Falstaff. He has lands and beefs, while Sir John has no more than the clothes he stands in and the bribes in his pocket. But to Shallow, Falstaff's town wisdom makes him a great man. Lands and beefs are nothing to a man if he cannot boast that he once spent a night in the Windmill with Jane Nightwork; and Shallow naively imagines that he puts himself on a level with the fat knight by this reminiscence, not realizing that the essence of Falstaff–his strength and his weakness–is that he would sell off every last ounce of beef and mortgage every last foot of land rather than miss a day's drinking or a night's drabbing.

There is no greater comic creation in English literature than Falstaff. He does not have the funniest individual lines, nor does he do or endure the funniest things. But he epitomises irresponsible laughter. We can enjoy his company but also at times disapprove of him, and so laugh at him with an easy conscience; and this derisive laughter eases any twinge of residual English Puritanism that is reproving us for enjoying the company of such a sybarite. Falstaff's undisguised corruption actually makes him the best company for merriment.

The second tetralogy of histories contains more than Falstaff, of course. In *Richard II* Shakespeare shows a political sense developing beyond the chronological listing of events that had sufficed for his earlier histories. Now he recognises that historical politics posed actual problems, and he examines these on a large scale and from a majestic viewpoint.

The central problem Shakespeare, the good monarchist, faces is the potential conflict between the rights of an anointed (and thus divinely approved) king, and the needs of the realm if a usurper could provide better government. Richard is capricious, irresponsible, greedy, extravagant, and growing ever more tyrannical. But he is the true king, by descent and by the oaths of loyalty all his peers have sworn. Bolingbroke is competent and pretty straightforward. But he has no Divine Right to the kingship.

Once again, factual history is secondary. The events Shakespeare describes could be interpreted totally differently. Richard's reign may be seen as an oasis of culture in a barbaric medieval wilderness (Richard was, for example, the patron of Chaucer). Shakespeare prefers to make Richard's court merely decadent. John of Gaunt, the super-patriot of Shakespeare's play, was historically a normally selfish, ambitious grandee, not a noble royal uncle counselling moderation.

But Shakespeare needs these revisions and simplifications to outline his main problem: if the true king is a bad king, may the subject revolt? If a potentially good king has usurped his throne, what loyalty does the subject owe him? Will the realm enjoy the fruits of good government if it has obtained that government by unhallowed means?

These questions are not simple, and they are not answered with finality in the play. Mere dependence on the Will of God is shown to be inadequate. On the other hand, to base all one's policy on a calculation of *realpolitik* is to remove the basis on which one might claim loyalty for oneself. Bolingbroke is an astute politician, but having broken his own oath of loyalty to Richard and trapped him into an abdication which is not compatible with anyone's view of the religious nature of kingship, how can Bolingbroke expect his companions in crime to be bound by their oaths of loyalty to his own sovereignty?

And so in the *Henry IV* plays, the strong, politically skilful king is shown being slowly worn out by the constant need to exert his political skill and military strength to retain his power. The final end of his usurpation is, of course, to be the anarchic Wars of the Roses. But Shakespeare had already written of that conclusion in his first tetralogy. Now he has an interlude of national prosperity to look forward to, in the reign of Henry V.

So he shows us the education of a great king in the princehood of Hal. As politic as his father, Hal knows that making himself look wayward as a youth will only

King Richard II.

enhance his dignity when he disappoints the fears that have surrounded the prospect of his accession. His historical age and Hotspur's are firmly altered: a dissolute adolescent and an elderly rebel are turned into young men with parallel careers. And through this contrast, Shakespeare makes the point that the glamorous pursuit of military honour and glory makes a rash politician.

In *Henry IV Part 2* Hal is contrasted with a yet more coolly calculating politician in his brother Prince John. Crushing a rebellion by sheer deceit highlights again the problems of feudal morality: what obligation does a loyal prince have to treat sinful rebels honestly? At the very least Prince John's actions are disturbing: we agree with Falstaff's view of him as a cold-blooded boy, and the contrast makes Hal's calculation the more acceptable.

Yet not everyone can stomach Hal's final rejection of Falstaff. The public humiliation of the old reprobate in what he took for his hour of triumph has seemed cruel to many of his admirers, even though moralists have firmly pointed out that no king could tolerate such a crony, and that Falstaff is already stooping to levels of dissipation and roguery that diminish our sympathy for him. Is it an evasion to suggest that this disagreement is a result of Shakespeare's lifelike writing? That he fills out so many aspects of complex personalities that we differ, as we should in life, over the moral interpretation of such a crucial incident? Well, at least as far as Falstaff is concerned it is easy to understand why some of his admirers will find that their sympathy outweighs their disapprobation, and others will not. But perhaps there is something a little too mechanical in the proposition that Hal consorts with his fat friend only that the sun may emerge in fuller splendour. Perhaps the dramatic shock of his casting off Falstaff with a severe lecture and a small pension appealed to Shakespeare too much for him to perceive the need to integrate it with a totally convincing individual personality for the young king.

It is different in *Henry V*. Whatever the reason, Shakespeare simply wrote Falstaff out of the series, and filled the comic centre of the stage with his lieutenant, Pistol. And however much we enjoy Pistol's antics, we always laugh at him and never with him. His bombastic language, imitated from stage conventions that were already distastefully old-fashioned to Shakespeare, distances him from our sympathy, and Henry can be presented as the perfect conquering king without our being distracted by regret for the isolation of the fat knight.

The perfect king is shown as one who unifies the nation. Hal's slumming had taught him something about the common people, and now, for the first time in Shakespeare, common people are portrayed without ridicule. The foot soldiers, Williams, Court and Bates, address their minds to yet another moral problem of

King Henry V.

feudalism: is a subject morally responsible for carrying out actions condemned by religion at the behest of his king? By limiting these actions to the violence of the battlefield, Shakespeare is able to make obedience the subject's first duty.

At the same time as he was writing the great sequence of histories, Shakespeare was writing the romantic comedies which, as Dr Johnson observed, seemed to come naturally to him, with nothing forced or strained. They are plays of a kind that no one else has written with anything approaching the same success. Their romantic element lies in a fairy-tale quality that may derive partly from the idyllic settings – Portia's Belmont, Navarre's park, the wood near Athens, or the Forest of Arden: and partly from the fantastic characters – the real fairies of *A Midsummer Night's Dream* and the pretended fairies of *The Merry Wives of Windsor*, the rustic mummers of *Love's Labour's Lost* and *A Midsummer Night's Dream*, the mingled shepherds and exiles of *As You Like It*. The romance is heightened by the sheer charm and good nature of the principals, and though their love affairs may seem tortured, the happy outcome is never in doubt. The plots are always airily impossible.

Such charm might have led to saccharine whimsicality and a silly, escapist irresponsibility. How did Shakespeare avoid these dangers?

A scene from a modern production of Shakespeare's sunniest play, As You Like It, *at Stratford-upon-Avon.*

Firstly, by allowing tiny edges of harsh reality to project into his plays: just sufficient to hint at a reef under his calm sea, though not usually enough to throw lines of foam over the sparkling water. Duke Frederick in *As You Like It*, for example, is a lightning sketch of a genuinely alarming neurotic. He is, as Le Beau says, 'humorous': his humours are disordered, and it is frighteningly uncertain what disposition will come uppermost in him at any given time. Orsino's enmity with Antonio is a consistent piece of reality, correcting the view that Illyria is a country where pleasant people inevitably get on well with one another. Gradually the moments of realistic tension intensified as Elizabeth's reign wore on: *Much Ado About Nothing* is jarred by the violence with which Claudio rejects Hero, and the last three comedies Shakespeare wrote before James's accession completely lacked the romantic glow of the wonderful comedies written in the 1590s.

Secondly, Shakespeare's lovers may sigh and suffer, but he never allows them to become wetly conventional stock figures. Silvius, in *As You Like It*, is, of course, just such an inert stereotype of formalized convention. But that is the point of him: the traditional pastoral lover is set up in contrast with the other couples, and needs the help of Rosalind's wit to carry him to the triumph of marriage.

For this is the period in which Shakespeare shows his delight in witty women. Rosaline, Portia, Beatrice and Rosalind are, above all, intelligent and lively. They sparkle. They never languish. We cannot fall yawning as they declare the depths of their feelings: they are more aware than we that it is very boring to listen to outpourings of emotion unless one is in love oneself. And so they mock themselves, their lovers, and us. They maintain a constant barrage of mental teasing, that in Rosalind's case becomes amorous teasing, too. Viola, nearest of the heroines to a sighing lover, is distanced by being required to make love at one remove, to and through another woman.

The love in these comedies is no inertly pure emotion. It is well salted with sex, and few of the heroines are above turning a naughty joke with a presentable young man. Often they have maids or attendants, like Nerissa and Maria, whose conversation may be a touch more salty. And low comic women like Jacquinetta and Audrey, can actually fall, or slip into *double entendre* suggesting that they have done so, without attracting serious condemnation: rather they assure us that in youth, the heyday in the blood is healthily present, and some lucky girls can gratify it.

Finally, sugary artificiality is avoided by the sheer excellence of Shakespeare's poetry. His two long narrative poems, packed with artifice, and his entire sequence of sonnets, have contributed less to his reputation as a supreme lyrical poet than some of the great speeches in these comedies. Many are familiar from having been repeatedly extrapolated and anthologised, as though they were poems in their own right. Portia's 'The quality of mercy is not strained', Jacques's 'All the world's a stage', and Viola's 'Make me a willow cabin at your gate', are among the best known passages in Shakespeare.

But the fact that these set pieces, like operatic arias, are so excerptable should not make it seem that Shakespeare restricted his poetry to the grand occasion. He packed his recitative passages with the rich music of language, too. He could be as lyrical in short conversational bursts, which he charged with growing and expanding images:

Portia:
That light we see is burning in my hall:
How far that little candle throws his beams!
So shines a good deed in a naughty world.
Nerissa:
When the moon shone we did not see the candle.
Portia:
So doth the greater glory dim the less, –
A substitute shines brightly as a king
Until a king be by, and then his state
Empties itself, as doth an inland brook
Into the main of waters.

At the same time, the Shakespearean verse of these comedies may be pungent. Sharp moments of mustard can set off the smoothness and anticipated poeticism:

The crow doth sing as sweetly as the lark
When neither is attended: and I think
The nightingale if she should sing by day

When every goose is cackling, would be thought
No better a musician than the wren!

The wit may convey a disturbing beauty, almost akin to the extravagances of decadence:

This night methinks is but the daylight sick,
It looks a little paler.

It may have the homely vigour of dispute, with an energetic, bounding rhythm distinguishing it above the best realistic dramatic prose:

Gratiano:
Would he were gelt that had it for my part,
Since you do take it (love) so much at heart.
Portia:
A quarrel, ho, already! what's the matter?
Gratiano:
About a hoop of gold, a paltry ring
That she did give me, whose posy was
For all the world like cutler's poetry
Upon a knife, 'Love me, and leave me not.'

The density of Shakespeare's poetic variety may be judged from the fact that all the above quotations come in one scene, within a hundred lines of each other.

Meanwhile, the dramatist's name as a purely lyric poet was not forgotten. Editions of the narrative poems continued to appear, and in 1599 the printer William Jaggard brought out a volume which he entitled *The Passionate Pilgrim. By W. Shakespeare.* It contained twenty short poems, five of which were certainly Shakespeare's (two of his sonnets and three songs from *Love's Labour's Lost*); several of which were certainly by other people; and the remainder of which are probably not Shakespearean. The book was rapidly withdrawn, and its title-page replaced with one that no longer ascribed what were now described as *SONNETS To Sundry Notes of Music* to Shakespeare. It is quite possible that Shakespeare objected to his work and other people's being pirated and all ascribed to him. Strangely, Jaggard repeated the venture thirteen years later, and again ascribed the whole lot to Shakespeare. This time some new poems by Thomas Heywood had been added, and he protested strongly, observing that Shakespeare, too, was offended. Once again Jaggard had to withdraw his title-page, and substitute one that did not try to cash in on sweet Master Shakespeare's popularity with the younger sort.

The Globe

THE MOST important theatre in English theatrical history was planned in 1598 and erected in 1599. The most important commercial agreement in Shakespeare's life was associated with it.

It started when old James Burbage died in 1597. He left the Blackfriars theatre to his son Richard, but this was a useless and, at the time, unusable legacy. Richard's brother Cuthbert retained the Theatre in Shoreditch, but the disputes with the ground landlord were increasing, and if the Burbages were to remain impresarios, they urgently needed another theatre.

The great decision they took was to associate the leading players with them as commercial partners, thus ruling out the exasperation of non-theatrical angels like old John Brayne, and giving the actors a stake in the business of the playhouse such as had only been enjoyed by Ned Alleyn in previous years.

There were seven shareholders in the plan for the new Globe theatre. Richard and Cuthbert Burbage held 50 per cent of the shares between them, and the remaining 50 per cent were divided equally between Shakespeare, Hemmings, Phillips, Pope and Kemp. Membership of this inner circle of shareholders, or 'housekeepers' as they called themselves, would henceforth be the most valuable position attainable in the Lord Chamberlain's Men.

A housekeeper was entitled to his proportion of that 50 per cent of takings that had always gone to the theatre owner. Of course, the Burbages still got two and a half times more apiece than did their fellows, but then they had probably put up more of the capital for the original investment. The site obtained was near the Rose on Bankside. And the materials were definitely Burbage property. They tore down the Theatre to build the Globe.

There were strong feelings in Shoreditch when the Burbages turned up to exploit that clause in their father's original lease entitling them to retain any building materials put into the site of the theatre. They brought with them a carpenter named Peter Street, and a dozen armed friends. Then

> throwing down the said Theatre in very outrageous, violent and riotous sort . . . did . . . also in most forcible and riotous manner take and carry away from thence all the wood and timber thereof unto the Bankside . . . and there erected a new playhouse with the said timber and wood.

Clearly it was just such a forceful commercial coup as had delighted young Richard when he defended his father's claims against his partner's relict. And with the profits shared, and the financial arrangements in Hemmings' capable hands, this made the fortunes – solid bourgeois prosperity – of the housekeepers.

Yet one of them resigned, just as the Globe came into existence. Will Kemp had more flamboyant ambitions than staying at the theatre counting the gatherers' takings. He proposed to dance from London to Norwich, thereby attracting great publicity, and perhaps making a fortune. He persuaded 'putters-out' – investors who backed promising ventures – to invest in his dance. Goodness knows what return they expected, but capitalism was not clearly understood even by its practitioners for another 150 years: investment, for an Elizabethan, combined bewildering aspects of usury, gambling, insurance, and merchant trading.

Kemp, then, was secure against loss, and left the Chamberlain's Men. His dance to Norwich did, in fact, prove a great success. He left England to dance some more on the continent, returning to act for the Earl of Worcester's Men in 1602. He had, in his own words, 'danced out of the world'. (The housekeepers were fond of referring obliquely to the Globe's standard, embroidered with Hercules bearing the world on his

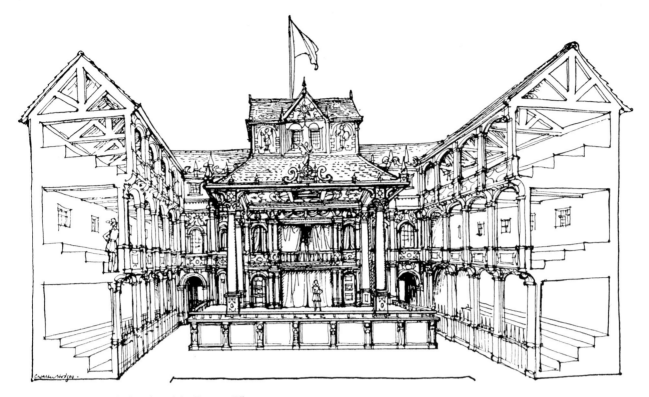

A reconstruction of the interior of the Fortune Theatre, Cripplegate. Although this theatre of Henslowe's was unusual in being square, in other respects it followed the structure of the Globe closely. From C. Walter Hodges' reconstruction in The Globe Restored. *By permission of the author and the Oxford University Press.*

The Bear Garden on Bankside. Unlike the theatres it has no huts rising above the seating galleries. This was the building that Henslowe controlled, and ultimately renamed the Hope Theatre in an attempt to combine drama and animal shows.

The Globe Playhouse, 1599–1613

A CONJECTURAL RECONSTRUCTION

KEY

- **AA** Main entrance
- **B** The Yard
- **CC** Entrances to lowest gallery
- **D** Entrances to staircase and upper galleries
- **E** Corridor serving the different sections of the middle gallery
- **F** Middle gallery ('Twopenny Rooms')
- **G** 'Gentlemen's Rooms' or 'Lords' Rooms'
- **H** The stage
- **J** The hanging being put up round the stage
- **K** The 'Hell' under the stage
- **L** The stage trap, leading down to the Hell
- **MM** Stage doors
- **N** Curtained 'place behind the stage'
- **O** Gallery above the stage, used as required sometimes by musicians, sometimes by spectators, and often as part of the play
- **P** Back-stage area (the tiring-house)
- **Q** Tiring-house door
- **R** Dressing-rooms
- **S** Wardrobe and storage
- **T** The hut housing the machine for lowering enthroned gods, etc., to the stage
- **U** The 'Heavens'
- **W** Hoisting the playhouse flag

The first Globe Theatre, in C. Walter Hodges'
reconstruction. By permission of the author and the
Oxford University Press, from The Globe Restored.

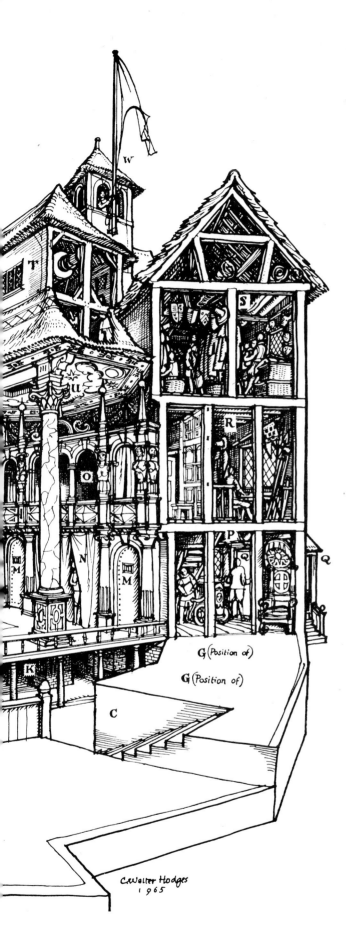

C.Walter Hodges
1965

Will Kemp dancing to Norwich, accompanied by a pipe and taborer. Notice the bells on his legs to give the morris dance jingle. From Kemps Nine Daies Wonder, *his account of his feat, published in 1600.*

Robert Armin in costume as the Clown in his own play The Two Maids of Moreclacke. *The long petticoat he wears is Elizabethan motley, a coarse cloth protective garment for fools, who were often mentally subnormal.*

THE

History of the two Maids of More-clacke,

With the life and simple maner of IOHN
in the Hospitall.

Played by the Children of the Kings
Maiesties Reuels.

Written by ROBERT ARMIN, seruant to the kings
most excellent Maiestie.

LONDON,
Printed by *N.O.* for *Thomas Archer,* and is to be sold at his
shop in Popes head Pallace, 1609.

ROBERT ARMIN,
was an Actor in Shakespears Plays.
See the list of Actors in the first Folio Edition.

London Pub Aprill 1.1796, by E Harding N°.132 Fleet Street.

shoulders). And he had finished his part in determining the nature of some Shakespearean roles.

He may, by his departure, have given Falstaff his quietus. It is perfectly certain that Shakespeare originally intended to include him in *Henry V*.

Evidently Shakespeare wrote at least part of a version in which Falstaff accompanied the army to France before replacing the fat knight with his stagestruck ancient. The change might have been made under pressure from Cobham. But it might equally have been made because Kemp had created the role, and it seemed so identified with him that the actors did not think anyone else would succeed in pleasing the public as Falstaff after Kemp's departure. If Falstaff was Kemp's role, it was surely his greatest contribution to the theatre, and it was daring writing on Shakespeare's part to give so complex a role with such psychological density to the clown who created Peter and Dogberry.

Kemp was replaced by an experienced comedian of quite a different kind. Robert Armin was more of an intellectual. He was himself a writer, and the most interesting of his works was *Fool Upon Fool or A Nest of Ninnies*, in which he described a number of great men's household fools or licensed jesters. This role, significantly, entered Shakespeare's writing as soon as Armin joined the company.

Touchstone in *As You Like It* still shows traces of Kemp's clownishness. But thereafter, the Armin fools reflect the strange 'bitter-sweetness' that was evidently Armin's striking contribution to the concept. Feste and Lavatch, in *Twelfth Night* and *All's Well That Ends Well* respectively, are comedians who can occasionally let slip the mask and show that they know themselves to be household servants and have personalities of their own beneath their motley. Lear's fool becomes a classic commentator: a voice of despairing worldly wisdom that conflicts strangely with his own unworldly loyalty. All these roles were created by an actor who had studied his subject, and knew that many fools were juvenile half-wits, desperately combining licensed effrontery and apologetic self-mockery in an effort to survive in a world they hardly understood. Their very 'motley' was in fact a useful pinafore, protecting them from the messiness engendered by their physical ineptitude rather than the pied medieval comic dancer's garb that stage tradition has handed down to us.

With Kemp's departure, Shakespeare and his fellow householders were made a little more prosperous, as they distributed his share between them. And now the company was settled in its membership under the patron who would give them their name until the end of Elizabeth's reign.

Insofar as their world admitted of entertainment stars, they were stars, and attracted their fans and their groupies. By 1602, students at the Middle Temple were telling a little story about Shakespeare and Burbage. It seemed that a lady from the city was so delighted by Burbage's manly figure on the stage that she arranged an assignation with him before leaving the theatre one afternoon. He was to identify himself at her house that night as 'Richard III'. But Shakespeare overheard the arrangement, hurried to the house before Burbage could get there, gained admittance with the pass-word, and – it must have been a dark night! – was in bed with the lady when Burbage arrived to announce himself as the hunchback king. To which Shakespeare sent back the historical information that 'William the Conqueror came before Richard III!'

Bear baiting in progress.

The Stratford Householder

Shakespear y Player by Garter

THE FIRST clear sign to Stratford-upon-Avon that Will Shakespeare was thriving in London came in October 1596. It must have been the successful actor who then reopened the proceedings to have his father granted a coat-of-arms. This time the claim to gentility was completed, and from 20 October 'the said John Shakespeare, Gentleman, and . . . his children, issue & posterity' were lawfully entitled to 'make demonstration of' a gold shield crossed by a black bend bearing a silver spear. Above it, as a crest, a falcon on a helmet shook another spear. The motto was *Non sanz droict*. 'Not without mustard!' grunted Ben Jonson in a play a couple of years later. He took a sturdily cynical view of clowns who thought that heraldry would turn them into superior beings.

But Shakespeare was of his time. The right to call himself 'Gentleman'; the right to be addressed as Mr Shakespeare; these were things that mattered to him. When in a few years time, questions would be asked of the College of Heralds about the propriety of these players being given grants of arms, the cock-and-bull stories of soldier-Shakespeares doing service to the crown a hundred years earlier that had bolstered the original claim would be revived, and Will's surer claim to minor gentility through his mother's family would also be noted. Perhaps, as an armigerous gentleman he began to satisfy himself that he was as 'gentle' as he seemed to everyone else. Perhaps.

The grant of arms came too late for one satisfaction. The 'issue and posterity' bearing the crest of the shaken spear would not bear the name from which it derived. Early in August, at the age of nine, Hamnet died.

Child mortality was, of course, common in that age of primitive quackery and overpraised herbal remedying. But no one can doubt that to a man of Shakespeare's sensitivity the loss was grievous. One does not have to endorse the sentimental Victorian proposition that doomed little Arthur in *King John* was created out of Shakespeare's grief. It is enough to note that in the character of Arthur, as in the character of Rutland in *Henry VI* and the little princes of *Richard III*, Shakespeare had shown how much precocious boyhood appealed to him. As he grew older, the relations between adult daughters and fathers would feature ever more prominently in his plays. But the treatment of young Macduff, and more especially, Mammilius in *The Winter's Tale* suggest that the recollection of a little son remained with Shakespeare to the end.

It is clear that Shakespeare's thoughts were much on Stratford, even as his career in London progressed apace. In the spring of 1597 he purchased the second largest house in town. New Place was built a hundred years earlier by Sir Hugh Clopton, up to Shakespeare's day, the most eminent scion Stratford had known: he had been Lord Mayor of London in 1492. In the 1560s, 'the great house' had passed out of the hands of the Clopton family and into the possession of that same William Bott whose deposition from the Aldermanic bench had made way for John Shakespeare's promotion. It was in New Place, rumour had it, that Bott had poisoned his daughter with ratsbane that he kept hidden under a green carpet.

By the time Shakespeare bought it, the house had passed from Bott into the hands of a family named Underhill. William Underhill was 'a subtle, covetous and crafty man' by one account. But his son, Fulke, was still more covetous and crafty. Shortly after Shakespeare's purchase of New Place, Fulke Underhill extracted from his father a promise that he should inherit all his lands, and promptly poisoned him. He was hanged at Warwick for this crime, and Shakespeare had to secure a warranty from a younger son, Hercules Underhill, that his own purchase had been properly made from the victim, and not arranged with the murderer.

The house cost him surprisingly little. £60 was inconsiderable for a building of its size. But the succession of covetous men who had owned it had allowed it to fall into a state of some disrepair. Shakespeare seems to have set about maintaining his new property, and thriftily sold the corporation a load of stone that proved surplus to his needs the following · year. He also, according to eighteenth century tradition, planted a mulberry tree in the garden. This proved so attractive to relic-hunting tourists that a late eighteenth-century owner felled it in exasperation, before his continuing annoyance that the house that had once been Shakespeare's could never be his own undisturbed dwelling led him to pull down New Place itself. The wood of the mulberry was bought by an enterprising carver, who turned out a vast quantity of cups and knick-knacks as profitable Shakespeare mementoes.

Master of his own house, an armigerous gentleman, a figure to reckon with in Stratford, Shakespeare might seem to have achieved all he could want in his provincial home. But he continued to look thriftily to his financial base. A series of bad harvests led to a good deal of hoarding by the rich, who could afford to wait for high prices to rise still further before releasing their corn on the market. Barley was being turned into malt, and then traded at shortage prices, and the poor were dangerously discontented at the way they were being exploited. In 1598 the Privy Council took note of this, and ordered the justices of the peace to find out how much corn and malt had been tucked away by 'wicked people in conditions more like to wolves or cormorants than to natural men'. South Warwickshire was one of the areas of acute shortage: still, in Stratford it transpired that there was very little wheat and almost no barley in store. But the wealthier citizens were doing very nicely with malt. Although no individual held a grossly inflated hoard, between them the prosperous bourgeoisie clearly owned much more than they needed. As a class, they had made a tidy little investment in a scarce commodity, and only a dozen men held more than William Shakespeare's ten quarters at New Place.

One of these was Richard Quiney, son of John Shakespeare's old friend and aldermanic colleague, Adrian. Richard was now a successful mercer who had been Bailiff in 1592. Now he held fourteen quarters of his own malt and seven that he said he was storing for Master Rafe Hubaud, and he and Shakespeare were

A ground plan of Stratford-on-Avon, made in 1759. All the features which would have been familiar to the Shakespeares are indicated.

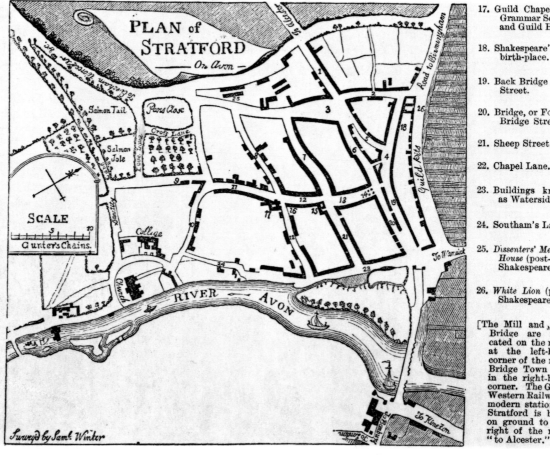

1. Greenhill Street, or Moor Town's End.

2. Henley Lane.

3. Rother Market.

4. Henley Street.

5. Meer Pool Lane.

6. Wood Street.

7. Ely Street, or Swine Street.

8. Scholar's Lane, or Tinker's Lane.

9. Bull Lane.

10. Old Town, where John Hall lived.

11. Church Street.

12. Chapel Street.

13. High Street.

14. Market Cross.

15. *Town Hall*—a post-Shakespearean building.

16. *New Place,* Shake-speare's House.

17. Guild Chapel, Grammar School and Guild Hall.

18. Shakespeare's birth-place.

19. Back Bridge Street.

20. Bridge, or Fore Bridge Street.

21. Sheep Street.

22. Chapel Lane.

23. Buildings known as Waterside.

24. Southam's Lane.

25. *Dissenters' Meeting House* (post-Shakespearean.)

26. *White Lion* (post-Shakespearean).

[The Mill and Mill Bridge are indicated on the river at the left-hand corner of the map. Bridge Town lies in the right-hand corner. The Great Western Railway's modern station at Stratford is built on ground to the right of the road "to Alcester."]

Shakespeare's birthplace. An illustration of 1769.

among those of whom a poor Stratfordian said bitterly, 'I hope, if God send my Lord of Essex down shortly, to see them hanged on gibbets at their own doors.'

Neither God nor the Privy Council sent any one to take punitive action, and Shakespeare continued to look for ways to make his money work for him. Abraham Sturley was Bailiff of Stratford in 1597, and a good friend of the Shakespeares and the Quineys. In January, 1598, Abraham told Richard Quiney of something old Adrian Quiney had recently heard about Will Shakespeare.

> It seemeth by him that our countryman, Mr Shakespeare, is willing to disburse some money upon some odd yardland or other at Shottery or near about us; he thinketh it a very fit pattern to move him to deal in the matter of our tithes. By the instructions you can give him thereof, and by the friends he can make therefore, we think it a fair mark for him to shoot at, and not unpossible to hit. It obtained would advance him in deed, and would do us much good.

Here is a fascinating picture of Shakespeare's native society. The search for reliable investments and investors is one that seems constantly to occupy these Stratford burghers. Shakespeare's mother-in-law had just died, so it is quite likely that it was Hewlands Farm that he was interested in buying, and that Sturley wrote off contemptuously as 'some odd yardland or other'. What Sturley hoped was that Shakespeare, if he had money to invest, would join a syndicate to buy up some tithes. The dissolution of the monasteries and the redistribution of church lands had not done away with the rights of the new owners to levy the tithes formerly paid to the church by tenants. But it was not always worth an individual's while to farm his own tithes, and so these rights could be sold to interested investors who could be sure of a steady

return. It was a gentlemanly investment, and in a few years Shakespeare would indeed buy tithes. For the moment, though, he bought neither tithes nor land at Shottery: he had a better investment to make in London in 1598.

In the autumn of that year, Richard Quiney travelled to London on behalf of the Stratford townsmen to request some relief of taxes in consideration of two disastrous fires suffered by the town. While there, he found himself pressed for ready cash to repay some local debts, and applied for help to Shakespeare. There was a good deal of borrowing and lending among the Stratford bourgeoisie: Abraham Sturley had just arranged to borrow £100 from a friend of his and Quiney's, but would have welcomed any loan of any ready sum from Quiney or Shakespeare in the interim. Quiney drafted a letter to Shakespeare which made no mention of Sturley, but

New Place, from a drawing in the margin of an 'ancient survey' made by order of Sir George Carew and found at Clopton in 1786.

pressed his own needs:

> Loving Countryman, I am bold of you as of a friend, craving your help with £30 upon Mr Bushell's & my security or Mr Mytton's with me. Mr Rosswell is not come to London as yet & I have especial cause. You shall Friend me much in helping me out of all the debts I owe in London, I thank god, & much quiet my mind which would not be indebted. I am now towards the Court in hope of answer for the dispatch of my Business. You shall neither lose credit nor money by me, the Lord willing, & now but persuade yourself so & I hope you shall not need to fear but with all hearty thankfulness I will hold my time & content your Friend, & if we Bargain farther you shall be the paymaster yourself. My time bids me hasten to an end & so I commit this to your care & hope of your help. I fear I shall not be back this night From the Court. Haste. The Lord be with you & with us all Amen. From the Bell in Carter Lane the 25 October 1598.
>
> > Yours in all kindness
> > Ryc. Quyney
>
> H[aste] To my Loving good Friend
> & countryman mr wm
> Shakespeare

That is the only piece of Shakespeare's correspondence to have survived. And it almost certainly did so because it was never delivered.

Before reaching the court to raise Stratford's affairs, Quiney seems to have encountered Shakespeare personally, settled his loan business satisfactorily, and also taken the opportunity to raise the question of cash for investment which so exercised Sturley. The same night he wrote to Sturley of the outcome, and Sturley replied within a week:

> Yr letter of the 25 of October came to my hands the last of the same at night per Greenway, which imported . . . that our countryman Mr Wm. Shak. would procure us money, which I will like of as I shall hear when, and where, and how; and I pray let not go that occasion if it may sort to any indifferent conditions. Also that if money might be had for 30 or £40, a lease, &c., might be procured. Oh how can you make doubt of money; who will not bear 30 or £40 towards such a match?

Maybe Shakespeare refused in the end. He had clearly not been as precise in committing himself to join the investment consortium as Sturley would have liked.

And certainly it is wonderful to see how the businessmen of Stratford swooped when they heard of the possibility that someone might be interested in a little profit. Crossing Richard Quiney's letter to Sturley came one from his loving father Adrian, suggesting that Master Shakespeare's money, and anything else that Richard could scrape together in London, might be put into a little thing that promised quicker returns than Master Sturley's lease.

> If you bargain with Mr. Sha.. or receive money therefore, bring your money home with you if you may, I see how knit stockings be sold, there is great buying of them at Evesham. Edward Wheat and Harry, your brother man, were both at Evesham this day se[ve]n[ight]t, and, as I heard, bestow £20 there in knit hosings, wherefore I think you may do good, if you can have money.

By 1601, Shakespeare was ready to invest in land. He bought from the richest man in town, John Combe, whose moneylending at 10 per cent interest had earned him the only house in Stratford larger than New Place. From John and his uncle William, Shakespeare bought 107 acres of arable land, with grazing rights in common pasture, and 20 acres of private pasture. This cost him £320. He could by now be described as a rich man. He did not intend to take up farming himself, and he let his new property to tenant farmers John and Lewis Hickocks.

In September 1601 he grew a little richer by inheritance. Shortly after Richard Quiney had taken office as Bailiff for the second time, old John Shakespeare died. He was buried inside the parish church as became a former Alderman, and the householder of New Place became also the owner of the Henley Street property. Half of it he let to his sister Joan. The other half was rented by Lewis Hickocks, who thus became Shakespeare's tenant twice over. Within a few years, Hickocks had turned his half of the Henley Street house into the Maidenhead Inn.

Very shortly after his father's death, Shakespeare extended his possessions at New Place, buying a quarter-acre of garden and a small cottage in Chapel Lane, opposite the New Place garden. He apparently wanted the cottage to house a servant.

Shakespeare's last and largest investment in Warwickshire was made in 1605. In that year he bought a half interest in the lease of tithes of corn, grain, blade and hay, from Old Stratford, Bishopton and Welcombe, where he already owned land. The vendor was Master Rafe Hubaud, whose malt Richard Quiney had stored during the shortage. The cost was £440 down and an annual rent of £22. But the guaranteed return was £60 a year.

He had house and land in Stratford, and his investments yielded a satisfactory income. By the time he was forty, Shakespeare could look at his possessions in his home town, with the comfortable assurance that he could retire there whenever he chose.

William Shakespeare, the Chandos portrait in the
National Portrait Gallery. The ownership of this has
been traced to Sir William Davenant, who claimed to be
Shakespeare's godson. The most likely artist – if the
portrait is contemporary – is Richard Burbage.

Essex and Shakespeare

THE APPOINTMENT of Sir William Cecil to the Council she inherited from Mary had been Elizabeth's first act on acceding to the throne. Cecil was loyal and cautious: a Protestant moderate fully as dedicated as Elizabeth herself to avoiding idealistic policies that might stir up hostility abroad and subversion at home. Created Lord Burghley in 1571, he became Elizabeth's principal minister of state, and shaped the political identity of England as a Protestant outpost that would always strive to inhibit any imbalance of power on the continent.

But if Burghley's intelligence contributed largely to this, his personality added nothing to the glamour of the reign. Nor was the son he groomed as his successor a more dazzling figure. Sir Robert Cecil was small and misshapen. Like his father, he had the prudence and diplomacy that Elizabeth needed and valued. But, again like his father, he lacked the aggressive masculinity to appeal to his Queen's intensely feminine nature, or to attach passionate supporters to his side.

The bravura colour of the reign was supplied by the courtiers, soldiers and sailors who became Elizabeth's personal favourites, and who urged more adventurous policies on the Queen and the Cecils. Sir Walter Raleigh was really a spent force by the late 1590s. His marriage to Elizabeth Throckmorton had lost him the Queen's favour in 1592. His lack of high lineage debarred him from easy access to the Privy Council, and he had to be content with the post of Captain of the Queen's Guard, and command of parts of the raiding expeditions sent against Spain. Yet those who believed he offered a viable alternative to Cecilian caution were not bedazzled by empty swagger. He was a competent military leader, a forceful intellectual poet and writer, and a political projector with the intelligence to realize that colonization was the policy that harnessed adventure securely to commercial gain. He was unfortunate that pioneer colonization is difficult and expensive, and the early

returns are normally poor. The Virginia colonies had not proved a tangible success, and Raleigh was not able to persuade other people that his dream of Guyana justified further adventuring in South America. His hopeless belief in a still conquerable land of gold on the Spanish mainland would ultimately lead to his death.

The principal effective opposition came from the faction of the Earl of Essex. He was young, handsome and brave; an enthusiastic rather than a successful soldier. He chafed at the restraint urged by Elizabeth and Cecil, and wanted to win glory for himself by fighting the Spanish directly. His highest point of success was his command of the raid on Cadiz in 1596, although it was actually Raleigh whose military skills ensured that triumph. The expedition to the Azores under their joint command was a contrasting failure, and the two quarrelled furiously.

Essex was unfortunately untalented. His good looks, charm and aristocratic descent carried him to his high position, and he never appreciated the political wisdom that caused others to question his enthusiastic proposals. His youth and verve won him friends and supporters, and the populace was always willing to cheer on the handsome hero.

He brought about his own downfall in 1598. O'Neill's rising in Ulster had smouldered for three years, when it suddenly spread violently and reached Munster. Many English, including the poet Edmund Spenser, were driven out of Ireland at great personal loss. The Council saw that the situation must be retrieved fast, but Essex was unwilling to let anyone else be appointed to the prestigious command in Ireland. So Cecil offered it to him, and he accepted the poisoned chalice.

Of course, he was totally unfitted for the job. For seven months in 1599 he committed strategic follies and allowed O'Neill to strengthen his hold over the disaffected territories. At his very lowest ebb, he held a

Robert Cecil, Burghley's son and successor as Elizabeth's chief minister. As Lord Cranbourne and the Earl of Salisbury he continued to serve King James. The Essex faction nicknamed him 'Gobbo', and it has been suggested that this was a joke arising from their familiarity with The Merchant of Venice. *It is more likely, though, that it refers to his slight deformity,* gobbo *being Italian for hunchback.*

long conversation under a flag of truce with O'Neill, in which they discussed the political consequences of Elizabeth's death, and Essex revealed that he was already in correspondence with her probable successor, James VI of Scotland.

This was treason. O'Neill was a declared enemy of England, in arms against Essex's sovereign, and Essex had no right to discuss anything but battlefield arrangements or surrender with such a man. Worse still, the arrangements made to keep the conversation private failed, and word got out that the Earl of Essex had talked treasonably with the rebel he was supposed to be suppressing.

With reckless desperation, Essex deserted his expedition, raced back to London, and forced his presence on the Queen who was not even dressed for receiving him. (And the elderly Elizabeth had the deepest objection to being seen before her elaborate toilette was complete). It

was the end of his power and influence. He was not punished for his failure and criminality. But he was banished from court, and passed the remainder of his life as the focal point of the worst kinds of sullen and hopeless disaffection.

Essex himself leaned to Puritanism. But he gathered Puritan and Catholic extremists alike around him, all hoping that the bold young man would make something more exciting happen than was likely under Elizabeth and Cecil. Essex became increasingly bitter against the Queen, and said that she 'being now an old woman, was no less crooked in mind than she was in carcass'. At last, in January 1601, he planned a mad *coup d'état*. Exactly what he hoped to achieve is uncertain, but it is unlikely that, had he succeeded, he could have left Elizabeth on the throne, however much he might swear after the event that all he wanted to do was to free her of the 'atheists and caterpillars' (Raleigh and his friends) who surrounded her.

Essex thought he could count on the support of more than a hundred prominent men to support him, including the Earls of Southampton and Rutland, and Francis Bacon. In the event, the two earls were among the very few supporters who remained loyal, while Bacon earned peculiar contempt from everyone for the slimy wriggle by which he transferred himself quickly to the winning side and joined Essex's prosecutors.

Raleigh, looking more serious than in the Hilliard miniature. As Captain of the Guard he was obliged to preside at the execution of Essex, his personal enemy.

Above : Richard Burbage, the great actor portrayed by himself. From the painting in Dulwich College.

Top : London, 1600. This panorama by the Dutchman, Claes Jansz Visscher, was not published until 1616. It shows what purports to be the first Globe Theatre – but the date of publication came after that theatre had been destroyed by fire in 1613, and the first Globe stood a little farther to the south-east, away from the river. From the original in the British Museum.

TOTO ORBE CELEBERRIMVM

*The Earl of Southampton in the
Tower, where he stayed a
prisoner for his part in Essex's
rising until the accession of
James I. From an oil painting by
John Critz the Elder, c. 1601–3,
Boughton House,
Northamptonshire. By permission
of the Duke of Buccleuch and
Queensberry.*

On Sunday, 9 February, the Council, who were well aware of Essex's goings-on, sent a deputation to Essex House in the Strand, asking him to explain himself. Essex promptly locked up the deputation to hold as hostages, and rode off with Southampton and a few followers to raise the City. Alas, Cecil had outsmarted him by notifying the Lord Mayor that Essex was a proclaimed traitor against whom the trained bands of citizen militia should be used, and the two earls had to make their way with difficulty back down Ludgate Hill to Essex House. There they found that many of their supporters had slipped away, and the hostages been released. Soon Essex was under arrest, and with all possible expedition he was tried before his peers, and inevitably executed.

It is highly probable that Shakespeare was sympathetic to the Essex faction, and certain that his work was

familiar to their chiefs. Southampton, of course, had been his patron. And Southampton was Essex's principal lieutenant and extremely fortunate not to suffer death with his leader in 1601. Elizabeth spared him, probably because of his youthful appearance, and possibly because she did not want his title to die out while he was childless. But he was kept in the Tower for the remainder of her reign.

Shakespeare, like so many others, may have thought that Essex's flamboyant posturing represented a lion-hearted determination to seize glory for England. He was, after all, a man of the theatre. There is nothing in his plays to suggest that he was alive to the limited value of dramatic political gestures; nor would the grand overview he had taken of England's history fit him to be particularly appreciative of the virtue of flexible negotiations within a limited set of options.

His one clear reference to Essex comes in the penultimate Chorus of *Henry V*, anticipating the citizens welcoming home of the victor of Agincourt are compared with the triumphant return from Ireland anticipated for Essex:

Colonists landing in Virginia. Raleigh's colonial enterprise was not an immediate success but the quality of adventure represented by men like him was lacking in the cautious politics the later years of which marked Queen Elizabeth's reign.

Francis Bacon, the brilliant lawyer whose desertion of Essex secured his own standing with the government, but damaged his reputation as a man. His essays were dignified, and his grasp of the 'new learning' gave an impetus to the age of scientific knowledge we inherit. But his personal peculations led to his downfall under James I. He definitely did not have any hand in writing Shakespeare's plays.

Were now the general of our gracious empress,
As in good time he may, from Ireland coming,
Bringing rebellion broached upon his sword,
How many would the peaceful city quit
To welcome him!

In a few months time, that patriotic gesture would be an ironic reminder of the hope Essex had once inspired. But in the spring of 1599 it was true enough that Essex's departure attracted enthusiastic crowds:

In all . . . places and in the fields the people
pressed exceedingly to behold him, especially
in the highways, for more than four miles
space, crying out saying, 'God bless your
lordship! God preserve your honour.'

Essex's attraction of this kind of public acclaim always galled Elizabeth and the Cecils, who knew that he enjoyed its underlining their own comparative unpopularity. Did this example of great popularity and a gracious public manner come into Shakespeare's mind, when he wrote about a similar man? He describes something very much after Essex's style in recalling one who

Mounted upon a hot and fiery steed
Which his aspiring rider seem'd to know,
With slow and stately pace kept on his course,
Whilst all tongues cried, 'God save thee,

Bolingbroke!'

Certainly, in writing a play about Bolingbroke's overthrow of Richard II at all, Shakespeare was hardly pleasing the government. Elizabeth would have preferred her subjects not to think it was *possible* for a divinely ordained monarch to abdicate, and until her death it was impossible for the play to be printed with the abdication scene included.

And how did Shakespeare have Bolingbroke explain his armed invasion of England? 'I have sworn to weed and pluck away,' he says, 'Bushy, Bagot, and their complices, The caterpillars of the commonwealth.' The play antedates Essex's subversive discontent. But three years later he was to give a strikingly similar account of his actions in similar language.

Lord Monteagle, a supporter of the Earl of Essex. He was one of the party who commissioned a special performance of Richard II *at the Globe in 1601.*

*Opposite, top: James I's queen, Anne of Denmark, a
pleasure-loving woman who used the resources of the court
to the full in her masques and balls. From the painting of
1617 by van Somer in the National Portrait Gallery.*

*Bottom: Henry, Prince of Wales. Like his father he
became patron of a theatre company, the former Admiral's
Men. His mother the queen was patron of the former
Pembroke's Men, and the theatre in England flourished
greatly. From the painting c. 1610 attributed to Robert
Peake in the National Portrait Gallery.*

*Below: King James I. His accession brought great
benefit to Shakespeare's company, who were granted a
royal patent and came under his direct patronage. From
the painting of 1621 by Mytens in the National Portrait
Gallery.*

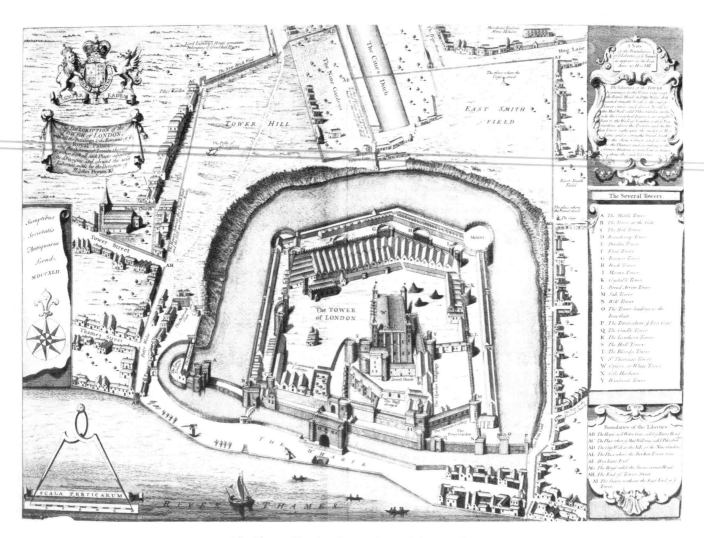

The Tower of London, from a plan made in 1597. Essex
was spared an execution on Tower Hill, the usual site,
and suffered death within its walls. Southampton
remained a prisoner until freed by James I.

The Essex factionalists definitely saw *Richard II* as their play. The day before Essex's rising, Sir Gelly Meyrick, his steward, ate at mid-day in Gunter's Tavern with several of the other conspirators, and in the afternoon took them across the river to see a performance of the play at the Globe. Two or three days earlier, Sir Charles Percy had gone with Lord Monteagle to see the players and arrange that the play on Saturday should definitely be *Richard II*. Augustine Phillips, who met them, protested that the play was so old and 'out of use' that it would not attract an audience. But the conspirators insisted, and offered to pay forty shillings to see the play of their choice. The players accepted the money and put on the play.

Elizabeth never doubted the reason. 'I am Richard II, know ye not that!' she stormed in her privy chamber. And, she fumed about the spreading disaffection it implied: 'This tragedy was played forty times in open streets and houses!'

The Lord Chamberlain's Men were lucky to escape unpunished. Phillips was examined under oath after the rising, and fortunately for him and the Company it was accepted that a bribe of forty shillings was sufficient to persuade any actors to put on a given play: they need not be suspected of subversion or foreknowledge of Essex's plans.

There was a brighter side to the Essex faction's interest in Shakespeare's histories. They were well aware of the Falstaff-Oldcastle-Cobham joke, and referred to it among themselves, and even to acquaintances outside their circle. In 1597, when Robert Cecil was clearly destined to succeed to his father's power and influence, Essex and Raleigh alike courted him. Essex, in a letter while Cecil was on a diplomatic mission in France, told him some of the latest gossip to pass on to a member of his ambassadorial retinue:

> I pray you recommend me also to Alex.
> Ratcliff and tell him for news his sister is
> married to S^r Jo. Falstaff.

The news was false. Margaret Ratcliffe never married. But it was notorious in court circles that Cobham wanted to marry her, and it amused Essex to tease a crony with the news that his sister was to marry an enemy.

Two years later there was more gossip about Cobham. This time it was Essex's cousin, newly married to Southampton, who passed the news on to her husband.

> All the good news I can send you that I think
> will make you merry is that Sir John Falstaff
> is, by his mistress Dame Pintpot, made father
> of a goodly miller's thumb, a boy that's all
> head and very little body. But this is a secret.

And a secret the identity of Cobham's mistress 'Dame Pintpot' has remained.

Whether or not he deliberately did so, Shakespeare served Essex's cause when he wrote *The Merchant of Venice*. Roderigo Lopez, a converted Portuguese Jew, was a physician whose services were transferred from the Earl of Leicester to the Queen. Early in the 1590s he made an enemy of Essex, who believed that Lopez had started the report that he suffered from venereal disease. In 1592, Lopez foolishly started to intrigue on behalf of Don Antonio, a pretender to the Portuguese throne. Essex uncovered the intrigue, and immediately cooked up a charge of treason, claiming that Lopez was plotting to poison both Don Antonio and the Queen.

The charge was successful. Lopez was tried in February 1594, and executed the same year. For those months Jews were topical, and Essex sought to increase the topicality that reflected glory on his supposed protection of the Queen. Marlowe's *The Jew of Malta* was revived successfully, and *The Merchant of Venice* was written as the Chamberlain's Men's answer to it. It is pleasing to note that even in this distasteful and deliberately anti-semitic piece of work, Shakespeare could not avoid giving the famous touches of humanity to his wicked Jew.

In 1601, Shakespeare contributed to a very curious volume called *Love's Martyr: or Rosaline's Complaint*. This speciously purported to be a translation from the Italian about the love of a Phoenix and a Turtle-dove. It further purported to be in celebration of a fashionable wedding. The author of the main, long, uncontrolled poem was one Robert Chester, but there were prefaced to it 'Divers Poetical Essays on the former subject; viz. the Turtle and Phoenix.' Two of these were by Ben Jonson; one each by Marston, Chapman and Shakespeare; and ten others cannot be ascribed.

It has been suggested that this strange collection actually represents a lament for the fall of Essex by those who felt that all beauty had left the state now that its hero was dead. Certainly the loss of Essex did engender a mood of national despondency. And certainly some extraordinary disguise would be necessary to permit any printed expression of regret to pass the government. And there is no doubt that Shakespeare makes far more of the quaint theme than can be easily explained if he had not some serious intent. The Essexian explanation of *The Phoenix and Turtle* is in some ways as appealing as in others it seems far-fetched.

Shakespeare takes the idea that Chester mangled, of a love between the Phoenix and Turtle-dove, from whose union springs a child to succeed them, and alters it to a lovely, mysterious celebration of a self-sacrificial love which, being chaste, dies without progeny. He opens with a summoning of the birds to play their part in the funeral, not unlike a more dignified 'Who Killed Cock Robin?' And he closes with a compelling threnody, simple in its rhyme, rhythm and syntax, yet demanding in its language and concepts.

Of his longer non-dramatic poems, this is likely to prove the most satisfying to a modern taste. It is challenging where the others are conventional; stark where they are ornamental; nearer to the indigestible than to the cloying.

GLOBE. SOUTHWARKE.

*The exterior of a Bankside theatre, after Visscher. The
placing on Visscher's panorama published in 1616
suggests that it was in fact the Rose Theatre, though
Visscher calls it the Globe.*

Top : Nicholas Hilliard's miniature, Unknown Man Clasping a Hand issuing from a Cloud, *1588. A recent theory suggests that the subject is Shakespeare at the age of twenty-four. Victoria and Albert Museum.*

Above : The interior of the second Globe, as realised by C. Walter Hodges. From Shakespeare's Second Globe, *by permission of the author and the Oxford University Press.*

Problem
Plays

THE DEATH of Essex, and the evident fact that the Queen was aging and would soon be succeeded, cast an unsettling mood of disappointment and expectation over the first years of the seventeenth century. In writing this was matched by a strangely *fin de siècle* tone which continued into the Jacobean period. In *Antonio's Revenge*, John Marston revived the morally uncomfortable revenge tragedy. Henry Chettle followed him with his frantic *The Revenge of Hoffman*. And Shakespeare opened the new century by making his own startling contribution to this revived fashion, in *Hamlet*.

From these plays, and from their successors later in the decade by John Webster and Cyril Tourneur, it is possible to list the conventions developed from Kyd's original work, which shaped audience expectations as they went to see tragedies of revenge. The hero's grief at some violent bereavement usually led him to dwell morbidly on thoughts of revenge until his wits turned, and he was likely to have at least one scene of raving madness. Often he attempted to check this decline by reading and meditating on the text *Vindicta Mihi*– 'Revenge is Mine, saith the Lord'. Always he would reject this Christian conclusion and determine on wreaking his own vengeance. Often he intensified his passion by avidly contemplating the body of a lover or relative he wished to avenge, or by gloating over the bodies of his own minor victims. A skull might be substituted for an entire body. The revenger was usually a malcontent exasperated that his services or abilities had not obtained him higher promotion at court. The victim he sought was normally of high or the highest rank, which made his assassination difficult. To this end the revenger would disguise himself, or assume a cloak of melancholy, and would arrange some court entertainment in the course of which swords (usually banned from the royal presence) could be turned on the tyrant. After all his bloody-minded plotting, the death of the revenger

at the hands of honest courtiers and survivors usually created marked relief of tension.

In the course of his plotting for revenge, the revenger was likely to be further aggrieved by discovering that his lover or one of his female relatives had been driven mad with grief over the crime he sought to avenge. Desperate suicide for love of one of the early victims was the common fate of revenge tragedy heroines. A ghost was usually at hand to prompt early thoughts of revenge, and would turn up as an avid spectator to watch the revenge carried out.

All these elements are found in *Hamlet*, yet examined in the context of other revenge plays they prove that Shakespeare was doing something quite extraordinary.

A modern Hamlet at the National Theatre. Albert Finney as the Prince of Denmark.

Hamlet and the Player King (Robert Eddison). A scene from Act III.

The intellectual puzzle he seems to have set himself was the writing of a revenge play in which all the familiar elements were turned topsy-turvy. Thus a ghost does appear, and does prompt Hamlet to revenge. But instead of reacting with instant, grief-stricken frenzy, and coming up sharply against Claudius's court security, Hamlet does what no other revenge hero ever contemplated – he tests the ghost's story! When the ghost reappears, it would be natural for the audience to expect that vengeance is about to happen: Gertrude will be killed, and the ghost will express his satisfaction at this just punishment of his adulterous traitress. But the ghost does just the opposite; checks Hamlet just as his rage against his mother seems growing uncontrollable; and redirects him to the more distant killing of Claudius.

Ophelia does indeed go mad; but not through any fault of Claudius's. Her grief is for her father Polonius, Hamlet's own, accidental first victim.

As for Hamlet the revenger, he does arrange an entertainment in the palace before Claudius, but not to kill him while he watches. As if to stress that this is unique among revengers' revels, he is given a unique opportunity after the 'mousetrap' play to kill the king at prayer, and he deliberately refuses it. Hamlet comes on stage, like many other revengers, reading a book. But whereas they invariably study gloomy Old Testament texts on revenge, Hamlet is extraordinarily reading and meditating on suicide! His morbid brooding does not drive him mad; in the only scenes where he apparently raves he knows a hawk from a handsaw very well, and is first amusing himself with Polonius, and later desperately covering under the mask of mania his crime in killing the old counsellor.

Hamlet is indeed a black-suited malcontent. But his black clothes are dutiful mourning garb for his father. And far from being a humble, self-made man, like most stage malcontents, he is malcontent from the very top of society, and constantly receives Claudius's awkward and embarrassed marks of consideration and favour. And when Hamlet picks up a skull, it is that of a man he barely knew, and leads him into a detached and witty contemplation of morality.

The very villain of the play is the least villainous figure to feature as a worthy object of Elizabethan revenge. Claudius neither sneers nor gloats. He is diplomatic, bonhomous and guilty.

The essence of *Hamlet* the play is, surely, that Shakespeare has written a revenge play without a traditional revenger as its hero. That he had done something extraordinary was apparent to his contemporaries. The minor poet Anthony Scoloker paid a most puzzling compliment to

> *Friendly Shakespeare's Tragedies*, where the *Comedian* rides, when the *Tragedian* stands on Tip-toe; Faith it should please all, like Prince *Hamlet*.

In praising a comic spirit that somehow dominates the play, Scoloker does not mean that Osric and the grave-diggers make a disproportionate contribution. What he is surely asserting here is that the wits of the audience were constantly teased by the perpetual, incongruous upsetting of conventional expectations, even while the humanity and situation of the characters caused their

*The monument of 1616 to William Shakespeare in the
chancel of Holy Trinity Church. His coat of arms can be
seen, surmounted by a symbol of death.*

emotions to be deeply engaged.

The important thing about Prince Hamlet is not that he is an intellectual, or unusually sensitive, or a procrastinator, or a man who could not make up his mind. For an Elizabethan, the most striking thing about Hamlet must have been that he was an ordinary man. Instead of the conventional figure, raging and cursing and raving at the expected stimuli, Hamlet teases his audience by showing how a man of flesh and blood might be expected to respond to the stock situations of revenge. Hamlet shows that a normal man would find ghostly visitation disturbing but by no means immediately convincing; that the revelation of the world's wickedness is more likely to prompt a man to thoughts of suicide than murder; that mundane occasions like watching an actor deliver a powerful speech, or seeing a foreign army cross one's country might be far more powerful stimulation to thoughts of avenging one's personal wrongs than the theatrical contemplation of a skull; that a melodramatic response to one's lover's funeral is a misplaced embarrassment to everyone, and must be expiated in untheatrical apology.

And, of course, Shakespeare's triumph in presenting an ordinary man in the revenge situation is that he keeps him innocent of the revenger's conspiratorial, murderous sin. Hamlet conspires to do no more than test the ghost's story. He does not kill Claudius until the *victim's* and not the revenger's plotting has introduced a naked sword into the royal presence. And he kills him without premeditation, when he has just seen before his eyes his mother drink a cup of poison prepared by the villain. This is hot-blooded and justifiable homicide. Flights of angels might, indeed, plausibly sing Hamlet to his rest, as they could no other revenger.

Another example of Shakespeare's mental pattern at this period is *Troilus and Cressida*. Here the comedian is indeed riding while the tragedian stands on tiptoe, and to such an extent that it proved impossible for contemporaries to slot the play neatly into one genre or the other. An edition of the play published in 1609 called it a 'History' on the title-page, and described it in an Introductory Epistle as the wittiest of Shakespeare's comedies. Yet Hemmings and Condell, who should have known their colleague's intentions, included it among the tragedies in the First Folio. What had Shakespeare done here?

He took a simple medieval love tragedy, an expansion on Homer that had been treated well by Chaucer and expanded again by Henryson. He retained the romantic passion of Troilus; the lovers' despair when political negotiations separate them by returning Cressida to her father in the Greek camp; her betrayal of Troilus with Diomedes; and Troilus' final grief. He inherited, too, from medieval tradition, Uncle Pandarus, the comic go-between whose prurient willingness to help young love

have its fling seems increasingly dishonorable as Cressida proceeds down the route to diseased whoring, which Henryson depicted as her final fate. Shakespeare slightly diminished both Cressida's and Pandarus' stature from the medieval tradition, and he may have intended Troilus' declarations of love to seem immature and bombastic. But none of this would be enough to rob the play of the force of tragedy.

The surprising comic element is one of satirical contempt for the traditional matter of Troy. In Shakespeare's play the Greeks are not heroes: they are tedious old men, arguing tortuously about how to get their champions on to the battlefield. The champions themselves are completely unadmirable. Ajax is a brainless lout; Achilles, a sneering queer, lolling in luxury with his catamite Patroclus, while his sinister bodyguard of Myrmidons provide the force to support his reputation. The death of Hector is a pivotal tragic moment in Homer, on which the fortune of Troy is seen to turn. In Shakespeare it is a vulgar, unheroic butchery.

Nor are the Trojans spared this satirical vision. Paris and Helen are shown as simpering and self-conscious. Their vanity is flattered by the endless killing their highly publicized love has caused, and they have no intention of trying to seek a truce and put an end to the bloody frame that so enhances their elegance. The other Trojans are forever arming and racing to 'the field' as if the war were a long-running football match.

Sullen contempt for traditional honour and the stable social order was widespread in the years 1600-1603. Essex had been as malcontent as Achilles; after his death, the populace sang laments for him until James's accession, and stubbornly refused to admit greatness or dignity in Elizabeth and the minister who had overthrown their favourite. Shakespeare, with his patron in prison and his standing in Stratford steadily growing, seems to have regarded the sophisticated centre of society with increasing distaste.

One other change of mood was apparent in *Troilus and Cressida*, as in *Hamlet*. Sexuality, which had been charming and delightful in *Romeo and Juliet* and the romantic comedies, now became matter for disgust. Thersites, the cynical commentating clown of *Troilus and Cressida*, sees no love but lust, despises those who are its slaves, and delights in describing the loathsome consequences of venereal disease. Hamlet, too, shows a thoroughly distasteful obsession with his mother's 'honeying and making love Over the nasty sty'. And this new attitude of sexual revulsion was to prove even stronger in the greater of the two comedies Shakespeare wrote in these years.

All's Well That Ends Well and *Measure for Measure* were the last comedies Shakespeare was to write for four years. Neither of them is very funny. Neither has the lyrical and ethereal beauty characteristic of his earlier comedy. Both draw upon the courtly romance tradition that normally supplied Shakespeare's comic main plots. Both admit to it a quantity of serious discussion that seems disproportionate to the fragile story, and in the case of *All's Well That Ends Well*, nobody has ever really felt that the resulting play is satisfactory.

All's Well That Ends Well carries to an extreme something threatened in *Much Ado About Nothing*. Claudio had been an immature hero in that play. Bertram, in *All's Well*, is a hero whose faults have painstakingly been drawn to outweigh his virtues. He is snobbish, ungrateful, a dishonest seducer, and nearly the catspaw of his empty braggart hanger-on Parolles. He has little to commend him but good looks and breeding. The play can never really get over the disparity between Bertram's function as an adored and desirable hero, and his character as an unfeeling young gallant. His rejected wife's use of the 'bed-trick' (pretending, under cover of darkness, to be another woman with whom he has arranged an assignation) is the conventional material of unrealistic romance (*pace* the law-students' belief that Shakespeare was himself an expert practitioner of this device). It is effective in engineering a reconciliation only at the level of plotting. Yet on to this fairy-tale world where all cats are grey in the dark Shakespeare incongruously grafts some quite serious examination of virginity, honour, unrequited love and loyalty. He had

come a long way from the idealization of *Love's Labour's Lost* and *The Merchant of Venice*, but had not yet found a satisfactory comic vehicle for his newfound suspicion of arrogant aristocrats and their vulgar parasites.

Measure for Measure took him a little further in the resolution of this problem. There is again a disparity between the mechanics of the plotting and the immensely serious investigation of human corruption in the seat of justice, the degenerating effect of legally tolerated sexual license, and the moral dilemma confronted by precisians whose consciences will not let them do commonplace wrongs to right larger evils. But the effectiveness of these serious elements has given the play its modern recognition. *Measure for Measure* is certainly a problem play in that it sets squarely before us some of the essential problems of life. Its comic structure makes little attempt to persuade us that they can be overcome by good will and subjective virtue: indeed, Shakespeare is at pains to show, by repeated twists of the plot, that a corrupt and powerful man administering justice has immense strength in his hands, and only such an implausibly godlike omnipresence as a disguised ruler who has witnessed everything from below can rescue the innocent in a wicked world. It will stand high in critical favour as long as critical taste wishes art to challenge us; it will seem more of a failure whenever it is felt that comedy should, above all, amuse and delight.

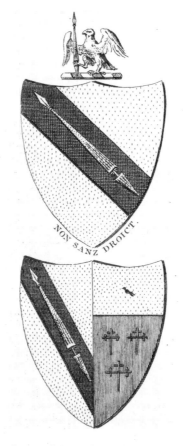

Shakespeare's coat of arms (above) shown quartered with those of Arden, below.

The King's Men

Palatium Regis prope Londinum vulgo White hall.

IN 1603 THE QUEEN at last died. Now, as the malcontents had hoped, new times began. James's progress south was marked by the extravagant number of knights he created. Elizabeth and Cecil had been very sparing of honours: Raleigh was still only a knight, and the great Lord Burghley had died a baron. Soon James would promote his son, Sir Robert, to Viscount Cranborne, and thereafter raise him again to Earl of Salisbury.

New men emerged: James pardoned and petted the surviving Essex conspirators. Southampton was released from the Tower and granted the revenue from sweet wines that had been the basis of Essex's fortune before his disgrace. Soon Southampton and Pembroke were both Knights of the Garter. Among others who rose on James's accession, the poet John Donne, disgraced under Elizabeth by an imprudent marriage, was persuaded by the King to enter the church, and swiftly became the court's favourite preacher and Dean of St Paul's.

The new court instantly set the pattern of Stuart extravagance. England was a far richer country than Scotland, and James had longed to enjoy the wealth of his new kingdom. His wife, Anne of Denmark, loved masques and balls. And so, among the beneficiaries of his very considerable generosity were the Lord Chamberlain's Men.

Within ten days of arriving in London, James ordered that Shakespeare's Company be granted a royal patent and come under his own direct patronage. The former Lord Chamberlain's Men were now the King's Men, and second in the list of members on their royal patent was William Shakespeare. The first on the list was another typical recipient of James's beneficence. Lawrence Fletcher had been the King's favourite actor in Scotland. He had to receive the perquisites of royal patronage in the new kingdom, and so, although Fletcher never acted with Shakespeare and his fellows, he was officially numbered among them.

Shakespeare was now, by virtue of this patronage, a Groom of the King's Chamber. He and his fellows were now secure against the harassment of the city fathers. Their royal patent entitled them to play 'within their now usual house called the Globe', 'as well for the recreation of our loving subjects as for our solace and pleasure when we shall think good to see them'. And they were now entitled to 'such former courtesies as hath been given to men of their place and quality'.

The royal favour came in good time. 1603 saw the most intense outbreak of plague in Shakespeare's

John Donne. He was sent to the Fleet prison by Elizabeth for an imprudent marriage in 1602, but he enjoyed the new monarch's favour.

*'The Garden of Plenty' arch designed by Stephen Harris
for the entry of King James and Queen Anne to London
in 1603.*

Mary, Countess of Pembroke, from the painting by Marcus Gheeraerts. A patroness of the arts, she was the sister of Sir Philip Sidney, and persuaded her son to bring the king to Wilton—ostensibly because Shakespeare's company was there to perform As You Like It—*but more probably to influence the king in the matter of Sir Walter Raleigh. Her son, the 3rd Earl, was the William Herbert identified by some as the Mr W. H. of the Sonnets.*

had been given four and a half yards of red cloth by the Master of the Great Wardrobe. His name headed the list of actors issued with cloth for this occasion.

In the summer Thomas Pope died, and three more actors were added to the Company. John Lowin became a very successful Falstaff in time. He was big and burly, and his commanding presence was not confined to comic roles. Tradition has it that Shakespeare coached him for the part of Henry VIII. The other two actors were promoted apprentices: Nicholas Tooley and Alexander Cooke.

The company was summoned to attend on the Spanish Ambassador in Somerset House in August, as James's peace conference implemented his remarkably advanced policy of stopping the war with Spain and seeking an era of peace and stability. In the autumn, James began his first season of extended Christmas revels, watching the King's Men in at least twelve performances, eight of which were of Shakespeare's plays. He saw *Othello* in the Banqueting House at Whitehall on 1 November, and *The Merry Wives of Windsor* three days later. *Measure for Measure* was performed on 26 December, and *The Comedy of Errors* was revived on the 28th. In January, *Love's Labour's Lost* and *Henry V* were mounted. Shrove Sunday was celebrated with *The Merchant of Venice*, which proved so appealing that it was 'Again Commanded by the King's Majesty' on Shrove Tuesday.

Wilton House, the home of the Earls of Pembroke. The drawing shows the original Tudor building, before the changes made by Inigo Jones.

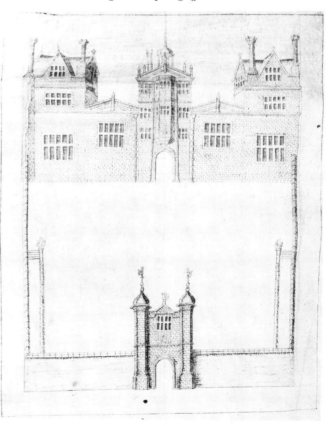

lifetime, and the theatres were inevitably closed. The King's Men were happy to find an engagement out of town, at Wilton House, the great country home of the Herberts. Here the King made a royal visit and watched them perform. It is probable that the play was *As You Like It*: a very plausible account is given by a reliable nineteenth-century scholar of having been told by the then Lady Herbert that a letter existed at Wilton in which Lady Pembroke urged her son to bring the King to Wilton to see *As You Like It* and added 'We have the man Shakespeare with us.' The Herberts' aim was not simply to amuse the King, but to urge Sir Walter Raleigh's case on him. Although the letter has not subsequently been found, the record survives of the King's Men being paid £30 on 3 December for having come down from Mortlake to entertain the King the previous day. The suspicious feature of the described missing letter lies in its inconsequential mention of Shakespeare, particularly as it was described at the height of the time when Pembroke was widely believed to be the Fair Youth of the sonnets.

In the spring the King was crowned, and Shakespeare as a Groom of the Chamber walked in the coronation procession through London, in a red livery for which he

An apology was necessary for one revival this season. Sir Walter Cope wrote to Cecil (by then Lord Cranborne)

> I have sent and been all this morning hunting for players, jugglers & such kind of Creatures, but find them hard to find, wherefore Leaving notes for them to seek me, Burbage is come, & says there is no new play that the queen hath not seen, but they have Revived an old one, Called *Love's Labour lost*, which for wit and mirth, he says, will please her exceedingly. And this is appointed to be played to Morrow night at my Lord of Southampton's, unless you send a writ to remove the Corpus Cum Causa to your house in the Strand. Burbage is my messenger Ready attending your pleasure.

And at one or other of the noblemen's houses, performed it was.

Although the gentry still had plays performed privately in their own houses, James's London was marked by an expansion in the number of theatres. Henslowe and Alleyn were not slow to realise that the building of the Globe gave the Chamberlain's Men an advantage over the Admiral's. There was also an obvious commercial disadvantage in placing both the leading companies in competition on Bankside, and leaving the pickings of the northern suburban audiences to be taken by inferior companies at the Curtain. Henslowe and Alleyn, therefore, engaged Peter Street to build them a new theatre in Shoreditch, specifying three times in the contract that he was to imitate what he had just done at the Globe, and once ordering that he make part of the frame larger than he had done at the Globe. The Fortune was original in being a square rather than a round theatre; in all other respects it seems to have been an undisguisedly copycat venture.

To this new playhouse, half a mile west of the Curtain, the Admiral's Men moved in 1600. Henslowe leased the Rose to Pembroke's Men and Worcester's Men. Two years later the latter company moved up to the Curtain, and absorbing what remained of Oxford's Men amalgamated with Pembroke's Men to become the third principal company.

The new Stuart monarchy extended royal patronage and protection to all three of the licensed companies performing when James came to England. The

John Lowin, who created the role of Henry VIII under Shakespeare's direction, and was a successful Falstaff in revivals of the Henry IV plays after he had joined the company.

Entries in the Revels Accounts of 1604–5 recording performances by the Kings Men of Henry V, Every Man Out of his Humour, Every Man in his Humour, The Merchant of Venice, The Spanish Maze, *and* The Merchant of Venice *repeated at the King's command. Under the column of poets, 'Shaxberd' is one of the more striking variants of Shakespeare.*

Admiral's Men came under the patronage of the Prince of Wales as Prince Henry's Men, and Pembroke's Men became the Queen's Men. And secure in Queen Anne's patronage, this company built themselves a new playhouse, the Red Bull in Clerkenwell, where they tried unsuccessfully to follow the example of the King's Men and avoid financial exploitation by making the leading members shareholders.

But the rivalry which most concerned Shakespeare in the early years of the new century was that of the revived Children's Companies, with their sophisticated writers, Jonson, Marston and Chapman.

The boys of St Paul's Cathedral Choir School had been acting before Elizabeth's accession, as had the Children of the Chapel Royal choir. Both these groups had been called upon to entertain at court, and had in the 1570s given public performances in the old Blackfriars theatre. As the sophistication of their writers was imitated by the adult companies, the boys gradually fell out of favour, and the Blackfriars theatre was no longer in use when Shakespeare first came to London.

But in 1600 Richard Burbage gave the Children a new lease of life. He had the lease of the unusable second Blackfriars theatre on his hands, and he let it to Henry Evans and Nathaniel Giles, who revived public performances by the Children of the Chapel Royal. The Children of St. Paul's were not slow to follow suit, and the court was sufficiently pleased with Jonson's plays to call back the Children's Companies to the Christmas Revels.

Shakespeare's company had to take note of the sophisticated, witty and musical entertainments that attracted the superior Blackfriars audiences, just across the river from their own playhouse. The children were having great success with Jonson and Marston's satires, and audiences were happy to hear the writers abusing each other in the 'War of the Theatres'. In Cambridge it was rumoured that Shakespeare had joined in, and given that 'pestilent fellow' Ben Jonson 'a purge'. But no one has succeeded in identifying with any certainty an attack on Ben Jonson in Shakespeare's work at this time.

Unfortunately the Masters of the Children of the Chapel proved themselves dangerously greedy in their wish to profit by their charges' acting, even at the expense of the singing which was their main function. Citizens who did not object to their sons serving as choristers for the royal family, had no intention of seeing them turned into harlotry players for the benefit of Nathaniel Giles! And the revelation that some of the Children of the Chapel were never employed in singing at all caused considerable scandal. The Children of the Chapel were reformed into the Children of the Queen's Revels, and for the rest of Shakespeare's career they remained somewhere on the theatrical scene, but never again the real commercial threat they had seemed when first revived.

These were the years in which Shakespeare's reputation as writer began to make its way into other men's writing. Chettle urged him, as 'the silver-tongued Melicert' to 'Drop from his honeyed muse one sable tear' for Queen Elizabeth's death. Chettle was never much of a writer: his mixture of black tears, silver tongues, and dripping muses is as messy as the plot of his surviving tragedy. And though he described the Queen as 'raped by that *Tarquin*, Death', he was unable to persuade Shakespeare to write any lamentation for Essex's avenging mistress.

Gabriel Harvey, whose posthumous attacks on Robert Greene provoked such ferocious responses from Nashe that the Archbishop of Canterbury stepped in in 1599 to burn their books and stop their pamphlet war, maintained a touch of donnish acid in the private note he inscribed in the margin of his Chaucer:

> The younger sort takes much delight in Shakespeare's *Venus and Adonis*: but his *Lucrece*, and his tragedy of *Hamlet, Prince of Denmark*, have it in them to please the wiser sort.

In a Cambridge students' play, the ridiculous Gullio demonstrates the erotic appeal of the narrative poems for the younger sort, as he raves on and on about 'sweet Master Shakespeare': 'O sweet Master Shakespeare! I'll have his picture in my study at the court,' he says, and

> Let this duncified world esteem of Spenser and Chaucer, I'll worship sweet Master Shakespeare, and to honour him will lay his *Venus and Adonis* under my pillow.

Belott

and Mountjoy

AROUND 1602, Shakespeare met a Huguenot tiremaker, or manufacturer of women's ornamental headdresses. Christopher Mountjoy carried on his business in a handsome two-storeyed building at the corner of Monkwell and Silver Streets in Cripplegate. His shop was on the ground floor, sheltered by a pentice which had been a feature of the house for forty years. Upstairs the Mountjoys lived under the pair of gables that covered their end of the building.

In 1604, Shakespeare was staying there with them. He may have been their lodger, having for some reason unknown moved back from the Bankside; he may simply

The palace of Whitehall, the scene of the presentation of a number of Shakespeare's plays.

have been their guest. But Joan Johnson, the Mountjoys' servant described him as 'one Mr Shakespeare that lay in the house'.

While he lay at Silver Street, Shakespeare became involved in the family affairs of the Mountjoys. Stephen Belott, the son of a French widow who had remarried one of the king's trumpeters, was Mountjoy's apprentice. He was, Mountjoy told Shakespeare, 'a very honest fellow', so that when he completed his apprenticeship, Mountjoy was only too pleased to take him into the shop as a regular journeyman. This too worked well. Shakespeare noticed that Belott 'did well and honestly behave himself', and decided that he 'was a very good and industrious servant in the said service'.

For the lucky apprentice, the traditional, folk-tale way

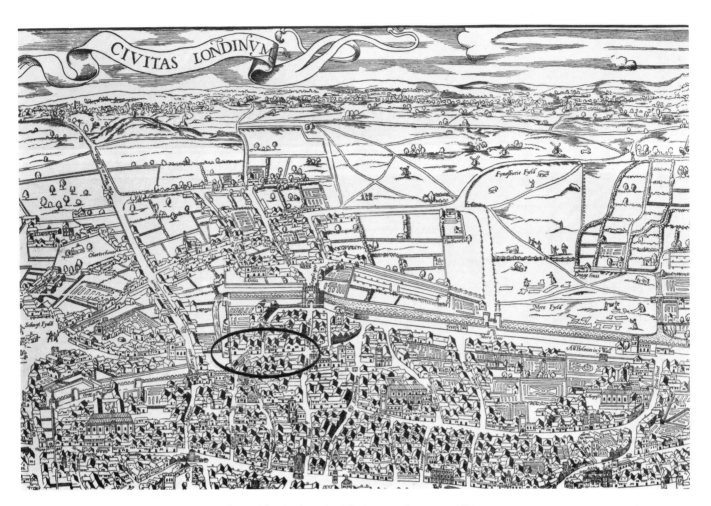

*Part of London in 1560. The house at the corner of Silver
and Mugle (Monkswell) Streets was still there in 1602,
when Shakespeare stayed with the Mountjoys. From
Ralph Agas' map of London, c. 1560.*

to succeed to his master's business was through marriage. The Mountjoys had a daughter, Mary, whom they wanted to see married, and whose future would be secured if Belott wanted to continue in the tiremaking business in Silver Street. Such marriages were fairly straightforward business undertakings. No one suggested that Mary and Stephen were devoted lovers. Everyone knew that the important question was the financial settlement. If Belott was to provide the security of his bread-winning for the girl, how much were the Mountjoys prepared to pay him for the service?

Mountjoy's first assumption was that it would be enough for Belott to reap the reward of the industrious apprentice: his master's daughter's hand, especially valuable as Mary was 'his sole child and daughter' and so his presumptive heir. But Belott was not prepared to enter marriage only to wait for Mountjoy's death before prosperity could reach him.

Then Mrs Mountjoy asked Shakespeare to intervene with the young man, and urge the marriage on him. Shakespeare agreed, and began to negotiate with the young man, taking to him Mountjoy's offers. These were an immediate sum of money, some household fittings,

and the promise of a substantial sum on Mountjoy's death.

The house was buzzing with the negotiations, and Shakespeare talked with several of the family's friends and neighbours of what was afoot. As far as they could gather, Belott was persuaded to accept Mary for something like £50 down, and some household furnishings. And Shakespeare's was the credit for persuading him. Every one was quite clear that nobody but Master Shakespeare had come to the final agreement with the young man.

By November it was all settled. On the 19th the young couple were married at St Olave's church, near to the shop. Did Shakespeare attend this wedding, for which he had played the role of decent, bourgeois Uncle Pandarus? No doubt he did, if he was well and in London and not otherwise engaged.

It was after Shakespeare's discreet assistance had brought about the wedding that the agreement began to crumble. The young Belotts decided against staying under her parental roof, and Stephen set up a separate shop of his own. Old Mountjoy gave him no more than £10, and household goods that Belott thought hopelessly inferior to what he had been promised. When Mrs Mountjoy died in 1606, the young couple moved back to enter into partnership with Christopher, but they soon quarrelled over money and moved out again.

By 1612 Belott heard that his father-in-law had decided to cut him off without any inheritance. So he started a suit against him, declaring that he had been promised £60 on marrying Mary (of which he had received no more than £10), and that it was also part of the agreement that he should receive £200 on Mountjoy's death.

Witnesses were called from among the friends and neighbours. Joan Johnson thought back to the great goings-on in her employers' house eight years earlier. Noel Mountjoy, Christopher's younger brother and his apprentice after Belott, gave his testimony. They agreed that Belott had been offered the good apprentice's reward: a sum of money and his master's daughter to wed. But none of them knew how *much* money. They thought they had heard Master Shakespeare mention £50 or thereabouts. But he alone had conducted the bargaining.

Master Shakespeare was summoned from Stratford where he was by then living. He confirmed everything the previous witnesses had said. Belott had been a good young man, whose services Mountjoy valued. But he was not prepared to put a monetary valuation on them: very carefully, Shakespeare testified that 'to his remembrance' he had 'not heard [Mountjoy] confess that he got any great profit and commodity by the service of the said [Belott]'.

But on the main point, the actual sum promised Belott, by which he had been persuaded to marry – ah, well! – there Shakespeare's memory simply failed him, and he was not prepared to swear to *any* precise sum. The key evidence on which the entire case depended was lacking, and it was Shakespeare who withheld it.

It has been suggested that his memory may have been weakening with age by 1612. He was then only 48, but he had only three more years to live. But taking into account all the testimony at the Mountjoy-Belott hearing, it seems to me more plausible to suggest that it shows Shakespeare's really extraordinary discretion. He was entrusted with a ticklish little family affair in 1604. He told the neighbours, but not in such a way as to make Belott look crudely as though he were selling himself into marriage. When testifying about events eight years later, he still had no wish to make enemies or be a party to any dispute. So he gave evidence that would neither offend nor assist either side. The careful observation that good though Shakespeare believed Belott's service to have been ('the honest fellow!') he would not go so far as to say that he remembered hearing Mountjoy claim that he had actually *profited* by it, suggests a caution worthy of Polonius. Clearly 'Gentle' Master Shakespeare had not lost any of the tact which so impressed Chettle twenty years earlier.

The quarrelling French tiremakers' case was passed by the court to the arbitration of the French church in London. The Huguenot elders and overseers upheld Belott's case in part, awarding him twenty nobles. But they were unable to force Mountjoy to pay. They also added that both Mountjoy and his son-in-law were debauched.

The Tragedies

BETWEEN 1604 and 1608 Shakespeare wrote his major tragedies and, for the time being, eschewed comedy completely. *Othello, Lear, Macbeth, Antony and Cleopatra, Coriolanus*: probably in that order they succeeded one another, with *Timon of Athens* proving dramatically intractable material and left unrevised and probably unperformed.

In 1599, after completing his English history cycle, Shakespeare had turned back to Roman history and taken the events surrounding Julius Caesar's assassination as matter for a historical tragedy. But, fine though *Julius Caesar* is, it has more in common with the histories than the great tragedies. It engages us through our interest in political forces, and permits us to watch the spectacle of changing fortunes in a struggle for power without overwhelming us with immense human grandeur enduring a dreadful decline.

Hamlet is frequently numbered among the great tragedies; yet I feel, myself, that critics who claim to be deeply moved by the play are less convincing than those who admit to being more coldly, intellectually engaged when watching it. Its virtual parody of the revenge form does not seem to me to admit of the deepest pathos.

But after James's accession, Shakespeare devoted himself for a few years to that work whose effect on us has been superbly described by A. C. Bradley:

> We seem to have before us a type of the mystery of the whole world, the tragic fact which extends far beyond the limits of tragedy. Everywhere, from the crushed rocks beneath our feet to the soul of man, we see power, intelligence, life and glory, which astound us and seem to call for our worship. And everywhere we see them perishing, devouring one another and destroying themselves, often with dreadful pain, as though they came into being for no other end.

How does Shakespearean tragedy achieve its great effect? Why has it seemed to men of different cultures and beliefs to be one of the greatest human achievements of the last four hundred years?

We must begin by asking the question that has engaged aesthetic philosophers since Aristotle: why on earth do we choose to watch – apparently enjoy watching – matter which is deliberately distressing?

It seems likely that tragedy and related art forms work for us by resolving some of the fears and tensions of actual life through a suggestion that the apparently meaningless or frightening elements in existence may be resolved to a comprehensible pattern, if not actually explained. Let us take an extreme case, and consider one of the most unpromising forms designed to evoke pity and terror – the commercial horror film. It has, of course, familiar elements of sadistic appeal. But it has, also, other morbid elements which might be expected to repel the most dedicated lover of cruelty. One does not feel that the Marquis de Sade himself would have gained any erotic thrill from elaborate maquillages of rotting or ulcerated faces, corrupt flesh, and exaggerated physical deformities. Yet audiences willingly go to be disgusted and repelled, and they do not seem to be composed of unpleasant psychotics.

I suggest that the appeal of this inferior art form is that it provides a consistent, conventional scheme, within which deeply frightening or disturbing aspects of life can be faced, and shown as having a place that is not merely random. The terribly disfigured face is, according to the conventions of the horror film, the evil work of the mad surgeon; the leprous hunchback *belongs* in the Ruritanian castle.

Inhumane as such work may be in discouraging us from taking a compassionate view of, say, goitrous imbeciles, it nonetheless satisfies our fears of a threat to our own identity in the very existence of disfigurement or

Hamlet and Horatio in the graveyard. From the painting by Eugene Delacroix.

little or nothing tragic about them: it was familiar reality, not ordered art, to consider that life was dismal for the depressed.

Medieval tragedy was not much concerned with moral values. The fall of a tyrant was as much a tragedy as the fall of a saint. Indeed, if the saintliness of the latter was stressed his history would cease to be tragic, and would instead be an edifying homily of a man dying in the expectation of salvation. But Shakespeare adds depth to his tragic pattern by the use of moral colour. The hero's fall may be a turn of Fortune's wheel, but there is nothing merely random about the chance that brings him down.

Typically, Shakespeare shows an evil external agent acting upon the hero and the forces of good, and causing them to make wrong decisions. Iago, Lady Macbeth, the three witches, Edmund, Goneril and Regan, and the Tribunes who oppose and inflame Coriolanus are such evil agents.

But equally typically, Shakespeare shows the hero himself abetting his own downfall through some moral

mental derangement. There will be no dispute that Shakespeare's tragic schemes or patterns are considerably more distinguished than the conventions of horror films. But to see how his tragedy works upon us, we must see what these patterns are.

The first tragic model Shakespeare inherited was the medieval concept of a turn of the wheel of fortune. To the medieval mind, a tragedy was the fall of a great man, whose greatness and decline were alike measured in purely material terms. In this sense, *Richard II*, *Richard III* and *King John* were all tragedies. The constant turns of fortune in the *Henry VI* plays made them tragic, and *Julius Caesar* showed the double turn of Brutus and Cassius overthrowing Caesar before being themselves overthrown.

This sense of tragedy is always present in Shakespeare. Fickle Fortune is constantly railed at in his plays: accused of 'feigning' and being 'an arrant whore'. It clearly lends dignity to his major tragedies that his heroes fall from some definite height, being kings or generals upon whom the state depends. This medieval sense of the fall from Fortune would have made Shakespeare incapable of appreciating much twentieth-century tragedy. The heroes of Eugene O'Neill or Samuel Beckett are down at the bottom of the turning wheel, with no hope of rising, before their plays even begin. Therefore, from the Shakespearean view there would be

The 'Pied Bull' edition of King Lear*; a version of the play, probably pirated by Butter from a source which is still disputed. But not nearly so flagrant a piracy as the 'Nathaniel Butter' edition, which has a similar title page and date, but no mention of the 'Pied Bull', and which was actually a deliberately disguised breach of Butter's copyright perpetrated by William Jaggard in 1619.*

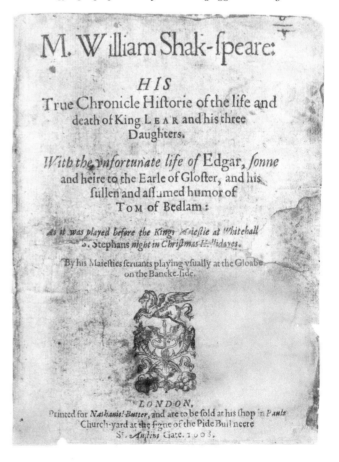

124

Laurence Olivier as Coriolanus. Stratford-upon-Avon, 1959.

is a figure of nobility; Lear is authority personified; Macbeth, Antony and Coriolanus courageous leaders of men. Yet as the plot entangles them, their moral stature starts to dwindle: they retain a theatrical and rhetorical dominance over us and the stage, but our sheer admiration for them lessens as their failings become more prominent. We watch Macbeth change before our eyes from a brave general to a frightened murderer, a sneaking conspirator, and at last, a superstitious, terrified, bloody tyrant. Othello's nobility crumbles as he allows his mind to dwell morbidly on Desdemona's imagined adultery, lets Iago persuade him to set traps for her and conspire murderously against Cassio, and finally suffocate his wife. To add the final turn of the screw to the moral decline, Shakespeare's tragic heroes are superbly articulate and acutely self-aware in some ways: they can describe their feelings in such a way that they seem to be passing judgement on themselves even as they alter for the worse (in complete contrast to the villains like Edmund and Iago, whose soliloquies are unemotional, conscienceless and self-serving). Catastrophe serves to bring Shakespeare's tragic heroes to a full awareness of their own moral collapse, and this too eases our sense that their death is harrowing; makes it seem rather a relief to them, and so to us.

It is, of course, an essential part of Shakespeare's tragic strategy that the dignity and nobility of his heroes should be thrown into relief by the ordinary worldliness, common humanity, and even absurdity of the characters around them. That inclusion of fools and clowns in tragedy which seemed to Augustan critics so clear a mark of his technical clumsiness, actually saved his plays from any touch of the frigid, lifeless loftiness that makes eighteenth-century heroic tragedy unreadable and unactable. When mundane characters react with elevated figures, the grandeur itself takes on flesh and blood. Lear can never be the remote, statuesque failure Tolstoy took him for while he calls his fool 'Boy', and is called 'Nuncle' in return.

The deaths of the great figures in Shakespeare's tragedies affect us as outrageous bereavement for ourselves. They themselves are ready to die: Antony, Cleopatra and Othello kill themselves. Macbeth goes into battle accepting his fate:

At least we'll die with harness on our back.

But if they accept their end, we do not. We did not ordain death, and we cannot afford to lose examples of human sublimity. Death receives 'a lass unparallel'd' in Cleopatra: we have to give her up. Our strong sense that these people have lived makes death seem an outrageously improper state for them, just as the death of an object of one's passionate love may seem unnatural. In our objection to these deaths we are, in fact, reacting against the course of nature, and the elemental universe is a part of experience that Shakespeare always involved

weakness which combines with external circumstances to ensure that his position becomes untenable. Othello's jealousy and credulity, Antony's luxurious love, Macbeth's ambition, Coriolanus's arrogance and Lear's vanity are such weaknesses – the 'tragic flaws' of Aristotelian theorists.

Given the combination of subjective and objective forces at play to bring about the tragedy, we watch a disaster being caused, and can neither simply blame the hero, nor simply feel pity for his being caught in the toils of evil. A tension mounts between our pity for him, and our exasperation with him for exacerbating his own situation. And this tension is relieved (we are finally forced to come down on the side of sympathy) when he dies.

This sense of tension is heightened by another form of moral patterning. Usually the hero is, in some way, morally admirable at the beginning of the play. Othello

The grisly aftermath of the Gunpowder Plot. The conspirators' attempted terrorism set back James's intended policy of religious toleration, and indirectly led to Shakespeare's attack on Jesuit equivocation in Macbeth.

in his tragedies, and that contributed profoundly to their grandeur.

It is most apparent in *King Lear*, where the rising storm parallels Lear's rising madness, so that the great insights into social injustice released by his ravings seem to come from outside and above human society, and also to reflect a general disorder and terrible lack of justice in the whole natural universe. Lear seems to speak for and of a cosmos in which, somehow, the concept of justice exists and is supremely attractive, while blind forces whose magnitude dwarfs the pettiness of human evil roll grandly on with a supreme unconcern for the fate of all living things, their victims. It is an account of experience – man, tiny but majestic, screaming defiance at the universe in the name of his vision of moral order, while that universe pitilessly overwhelms him – that has been most attractive to post-Christian cultures. *King Lear* has become more and more *the* Shakespearean tragedy for the twentieth century, though as recent a critic as Charles Lamb found its vision too devastating, and thought that the only actable version was a moralising eighteenth-century 'improvement' that rewarded the good characters and

punished the wicked.

But the superhuman elements are always present in Shakespeare's tragic account of humanity. A vision of hell lurks on the outer perimeter of *Macbeth*, and from the moment he listens willingly to the witches, Macbeth allows himself to be drawn further and further into the morass of nightmares and ghosts and bloody visions and lying prophecies. Antony's god drains away from him in a dribble of music under the stage. Yet in *Antony and Cleopatra* it is a human rather than a spiritual or natural element that manages to take on metaphysical power. The uncontrollable, passionate, experienced, lustful love that makes the pair youthful even when they are palpably middle-aged; that seems to them and to us to weigh well in the balance against the alternative of world empire; the transfiguring and destroying force of sexual passion is the godlike element that sweeps away reason and calculation, and makes the triumvir and his serpent of old Nile two of the finest representatives of *grande passion* in English literature.

Othello and *Coriolanus* rely upon language and imagery to lift us above the daily world of men. And repeatedly they do so lift us. Othello's jealous rage is as cold and unchanging as

> the Pontic sea,
> Whose icy current and compulsive course,
> Ne'er feels retiring ebb, but keeps due on
> To the Propontic, and the Hellespont.

Coriolanus combines a little piece of stage business from Shakespeare's pen, very human in its effect, with a speech that raises his situation to the cosmic, as he yields to his mother's entreaties to spare Rome, with the certainty that his Volscian allies will not, then, spare him:

> (*Holds her by the hand silent.*)
>   O mother, mother!
> What have you done? Behold, the heavens do ope,
> The gods look down, and this unnatural scene
> They laugh at.

And these short speeches, far from the most impressive in the tragedies, remind us that Shakespeare's poetic skill was not flagging: rather it was strengthening, improving, becoming metrically more free and flexible all the time, while its imagery steadily lost the hint of ornament, and became a means of expressing more precise meaning or deeper profundity than could be achieved by flat statement and pretty comparison. Other tragedians may well have had something of the grand cosmic vision of Shakespeare, or his quick sense of human sympathy. But the language in which to express these things with precision, force and unsentimentality is an even rarer gift than visionary insight. Shakespeare is England's *greatest* writer because he is England's greatest *writer*.

There is little scope for speculation about Shakespeare's life in the tragedies. The tone of sexual disgust that we noticed in the problem plays was retained in the earlier tragedies. It is present in *Othello* and *King Lear*, and while the sheer nausea thereafter decreases, there is never a return to the carefree combination of prettiness, sexuality and flirtation that was so marked in the romantic comedies. Cleopatra is an experienced temptress, and she does not exercise her wiles with impunity. And no heroine later than Beatrice was willing to make a jest of her own chastity. Helena in *All's Well That Ends Well*, was the last of Shakespeare's ladies to enjoy bawdy banter with men.

This development is so marked that it is reasonable to infer some biographical cause, even though the specific cause inferred must always be a guess. But a change in tone that cuts right across genres of comedy, tragedy and romance suggests something more than mere artistic experimentation. It has been speculated that Shakespeare might have himself contracted veneral disease around 1600, and slowly recovered from an initial disgust engendered by this misfortune. But it may be equally worth noting that he was the father of two adolescent daughters – Susanna was seventeen and Judith fifteen in 1600 – and they may have caused him some anxiety. Whatever the cause, Shakespeare certainly moved to a graver view of human sexuality as he entered middle age.

The most notable historical observation to be drawn from the tragedies is the marked flattery of James I in *Macbeth*, whose ancestor Banquo is portrayed kindly, with a prophetic vision of James's own rule over two kingdoms. And in the same play the Jesuit Provincial, Father Garnett, is indirectly attacked. He had shocked Catholics and Protestants alike by denying any knowledge of the Gunpowder Plot, and later claiming that this was morally acceptable equivocation. Elizabethans objected strongly to lying, and the drunken porter welcomes an equivocating Jesuit to Hell.

King Lear may possibly owe something to an acquaintance of the Southampton circle. After the death of the Earl's mother, Sir William Harvey remarried. His new wife was Cordell (or Cordelia) Annesley, and she had tried hard to prevent her two grasping older sisters from exploiting the senility of their father, Sir Brian, to have him certified insane, and seize his property.

Last Years in London

Two of Shakespeare's brothers followed him to London. Gilbert became a haberdasher in St Bridget's parish, and, like Shakespeare, kept up friendship and business ties in Stratford. He never married.

Neither did Edmund, who followed in his brother's professional as well as residential footsteps, and became an actor. Edmund was not, however without short-lived issue. In August 1607, the 'base-borne' child of 'Edward Shakespeare, Player' was buried at St Giles, Cripplegate.

In December of the same year Edmund followed his illegitimate son, and was buried in St Saviour's. It must have been William who went to the expense of giving him a funeral costing 20 shillings rather than the usual 3 shillings.

The following year saw the King's Men make an extremely important move. They recovered the lease of the Blackfriars Theatre. Once again, the inner circle were invited to become shareholders, and the two Burbages, Shakespeare, Hemmings, Condell, Sly and a representative of the former leaseholder, Henry Evans, became equal partners in the profits (Phillips had died in 1605). The only advantage retained by the Burbages this time was their £40 annual rent as landlords.

At last the King's Men had what old James Burbage had always wanted: their own summer quarters at the Globe on Bankside, and their own winter quarters indoors within the Liberty of Blackfriars. The 'little eyases' had inured the Blackfriars residents to the prospect of a theatre in their midst and, indeed, opposition to theatres was making less headway under James than had been possible under Elizabeth. The Puritans struck their last successful blow at the theatre in Shakespeare's lifetime by passing an act to ban swearing and blasphemy on the stage in 1606. It was a pinprick compared with the real threats mounted during Cobham's Lord Chamberlainship: the actors simply swore 'By Jove!' or 'By sky!' instead of 'By God!'

The change to the Blackfriars theatre had its effect on the sort of plays that were commercially viable. The fashionable residents of the Liberty liked masques and spectacle, and definitely enjoyed old fashioned romance. Now, since *The Two Gentlemen of Verona* – not one of his better pieces – Shakespeare had not attempted anything closer to the true, adventurous romance than the fairy magic of *A Midsummer Night's Dream* and the pastoral enchantment of *As You Like It*. He had preferred Italianate witty love tangles. Nor was his first attempt to meet the new fashion entirely successful. *Pericles, Prince of Tyre* suffers from the gravest defect to which romance is liable: it is a sheer hodge-podge of adventures, sailings-away, shipwrecks and fresh adventures. It is generally agreed that the work is not Shakespeare's in its entirety, but he wrote the last three acts, telling the story of Pericles' loss of his wife and daughter in a storm, and recovery of them years later, when he finds his daughter's virtue and chastity ruining trade in a brothel in a strange country, and his wife serving as a temple priestess.

The new mode perhaps demanded new men. Francis Beaumont and John Fletcher had written plays, separately and in collaboration, for the Children's Companies, and were in touch with fashionable taste. They now began to write for the King's Men. According to Restoration gossip, they lived in one house on the Bankside, sharing one cloak and one wench.

After his marriage in 1613, Beaumont abandoned writing for the theatre. But Fletcher went on to become the King's Men's replacement for Shakespeare as their principal writer, and collaborated with Shakespeare at least twice: on *Henry VIII* (mainly Shakespeare's) and *The Two Noble Kinsmen* (mainly Fletcher's). A lost play, *Cardenio*, probably came from their joint pens also.

Soon after the move to Blackfriars, William Sly died, and was buried back in London's earliest theatreland, Shoreditch. Two weeks after Sly, Lawrence Fletcher, the

John Fletcher, who collaborated with Shakespeare on
Henry VIII, The Two Noble Kinsmen *and the lost
play* Cardenio, *and succeeded him as principal writer
for the King's Men.*

*Francis Beaumont, who lived and collaborated with
Fletcher, but left writing for the theatre before
Shakespeare's retirement.*

King's Scottish favourite, also died. Their places were filled by maturing members of the Children's Company. Evans's removal from the Blackfriars had marked another change in the fortunes of the Children of the Revels, who now became the Children of Whitefriars, where they played in a far less salubrious environment. William Ostler and John Underwood were happy to leave them and become full members of the adult King's Men. The most successful of all the Child Actors, handsome, libertine Nathan Field, also graduated to becoming a King's Man, but only when Shakespeare's death left his place vacant.

By 1609, Shakespeare seems to have given serious thought to leaving London. His relative Thomas Greene, the town clerk of Stratford, was staying at New Place, and evidently expected to have to move out: he wrote of his reprieve in September, when he perceived that he 'might stay another year at New Place'. By 1612, Shakespeare had returned and Greene had left, though around this time the collaborative plays with Fletcher were written, showing that he did not feel all professional ties with the London theatre to be cut.

His fame was now more apparent in widespread productions of the plays than in references to his sweet poems. *Pericles* was performed by a company of recusants in Yorkshire. And some ships bound for the East Indies varied the autumn and spring of 1607-8 off the coast of Sierra Leone with performances of *Hamlet* and *Richard II* on board. Captain Keeling of the *Dragon* noted severely that he set his men to these exotically situated amateur theatricals 'to keep my people from idleness and unlawful games, or sleep'.

In the spring of 1611, Simon Forman wrote himself busy memoranda about plays he saw at the Globe. *Macbeth* impressed the old quack professionally:

> Observe also how Macbeth's queen did Rise
> in the night in her sleep, & walked and talked
> and confessed all, & the doctor noted her
> words

he wrote down. He liked hearing women's confidences himself, and this evidently struck a chord. He was impressed, too, by Autolycus in *The Winter's Tale*, and sharply memorialised himself to 'Beware of trusting feigned beggars or fawning fellows.' *Cymbeline* inspired him to nothing more than a plot synopsis.

The court was enjoying the new plays, too. *The Tempest* and *The Winter's Tale* were played before the King in November. And at the celebrations in February, when the Elector Palatine came over to marry James's daughter Elizabeth, there were new and old plays to be seen: *The Tempest, The Winter's Tale, Othello, Julius Caesar*, 'The Hotspur' and 'Sir John Falstaff' (presumably *Henry IV* parts 1 and 2, with Lowin as Falstaff), and *Much Ado About Nothing*, which proved sufficiently popular to bear repetition as *Beatrice and Benedick*.

John Gielgud as Prospero. Stratford-upon-Avon, 1957.

attracted wits and poets to regular evenings of conversation. While Shakespeare probably never met Raleigh there, and is unlikely to have dominated the company, his can safely be counted with the 'Shades of poets dead and gone' who assembled there.

On 29 March 1613 there was a tilt to celebrate the anniversary of the King's accession. The old chivalric military sport survived as a court entertainment. Its unreal nature was stressed by one aspect of the Jacobean contest. Before the tilting began, squires carried *Imprese* into the arena: cardboard shields painted with devices and mottoes for the contestants. They were not their real coats-of-arms, but decorations for the special occasions, and were themselves judged competitively for their wit and ingenuity.

Francis Manners, 6th Earl of Rutland, was, like the other surviving Protestant Essex men, back in court favour. He took part in this tilt, and turned to professionals to create his *impresa*. What his device was we do not know, but Shakespeare invented it and Burbage painted it. It was not the most highly acclaimed *impresa* at the tilt, but the two friends earned forty-four shillings apiece for their labours.

1613 was the year of disaster for the Globe, and probably terminated Shakespeare's professional asso-

Nathan Field, handsomest and most successful of the boy actors, who took Shakespeare's place as a King's Man on his death.

By now, as the Belott-Mountjoy hearings showed, Shakespeare was definitely resident in Stratford. But he maintained business interests in London. Three months before the hearings he was in London to buy the Blackfriars Gatehouse from a musician named Henry Walker. The building had once been part of the Prior's lodging, and was very close to the theatre. The purchase was an investment and Shakespeare let the house to one John Robinson.

In signing a mortgage to Walker, apparently as security for the payment of the last £60 of the purchase money, Shakespeare associated himself with three trustees. Hemmings was one of them. Another was a Yorkshireman named John Jackson. But the third was William Johnson, landlord of the Mermaid Tavern. This association with its landlord raises Shakespeare's traditional association with the Mermaid to the standing of virtual certainty. Beaumont, Fletcher, Jonson and Donne were certainly habitués of the tavern where Sir Walter Raleigh had started the Friday Street Club, and

ciation with his fellows. On 29 June his *Henry VIII* was being given a spectacular performance. The King's entry to Cardinal Wolsey's entertainment was heralded with the firing of chambers, and nobody noticed that one of the paper stoppers used as dummy shot had set fire to the thatch above. It was 'thought at first but an idle smoke', said Sir Henry Wotton. And so it spread round the wooden O, and in less than an hour, the theatre of Shakespeare was destroyed.

Fortunately no lives were lost. One man's breeches caught fire, but a joker put him out by pouring a bottle of beer over him. The actors rescued nearly all their costumes and properties, including, thank goodness, Shakespeare's scripts, most of which would otherwise have been lost to us.

Rebuilding began almost immediately, but Shakespeare does not seem to have joined the new arrangement of shareholders. Possibly he did not wish to put down the capital required, or be troubled with having his receipts sent from London to Stratford. But he probably did not wish his fellows to suffer from his 'shares being dissolved to strangers', for he left no theatre shares in his will.

The new Globe brought the other major company back to Bankside. Once again, Henslowe decided to compete with the rebuilders, and he set about converting the Bear Garden into a theatre fit for human or animal entertainments. Ben Jonson complained that this new Hope theatre stank like Smithfield, but it was successful enough to cause the final closure of the Swan and the Rose.

The timbers of the old Globe had been part of the first English theatre, and probably witnessed the performance of Shakespeare's first play. It was fitting that they should be destroyed in his last. He was a retired denizen of Stratford, and the glorious twenty years of Shakespearean creation were over.

Shakespeare's birthplace as it looks today.

The Last Plays

WE HAVE noted that the romance form was not easy, and *Pericles* failed to surmount its difficulties. It was popular in its own day, as we can see from its production in Yorkshire and its publication in quarto form. Hemmings and Condell, however, did not feel Shakespeare's part in it sufficient to warrant its inclusion in the Folio.

The most striking Shakespearean achievements in it are the extremely unpromising brothel scenes. The narrative idea seems ridiculous: a virtuous girl, captured by pirates, is sold to a bawd, but damages the trade by persuading all the customers sent to her to leave her alone and return to virtue. It ought to be a lamentable failure, but amazingly, Shakespeare succeeds in establishing a wonderful contrast between the scenes with the comically disgruntled bawd and her man, who wish to settle Marina once and for all by raping her, yet are loth to spoil the virginity that should set her price high; and the very restrained scene where Marina dissuades the disguised governor from carrying out his designs on her.

Cymbeline, too, suffers from confused plotting. Too many conspiracies, disguises and political threats are intertwined for reader or spectator to have a clear sense of what is going on all the time. Yet it contains beautiful poetry, and Imogen, the wife whose husband is tricked into believing she has been unfaithful to him, is one of Shakespeare's finest and most convincing heroines. In this play he began to realize the tragi-comic possibilities of the romance form. Instead of touching comedy with melancholy, he was able to set up situations which seemed inevitably to be leading to a tragic conclusion, and then succeeded in recovering an optimistic balance.

By a bold technical device he made *The Winter's Tale* achieve the perfection of tragi-comedy. The first three acts are directly tragic, and sweep irresistibly to a pathetic conclusion. Leontes' unfounded jealousy leads inexorably to the death of his son, the banishment and intended exposure of his baby daughter, and the apparent death of his queen.

The bold gesture comes at the end of Act III and the beginning of Act IV. The last death caused by Leontes' jealous tyranny, that of loyal Antigonus, charged with exposing the infant Perdita, takes on a ludicrous tinge, as he races off stage pursued by a bear, and his death and the wrecking of his ship, lamentable events both, are somewhat absurdly described by the young clown. Then Time steps in to introduce Act IV, proclaiming that

King Henry VIII, after Holbein.

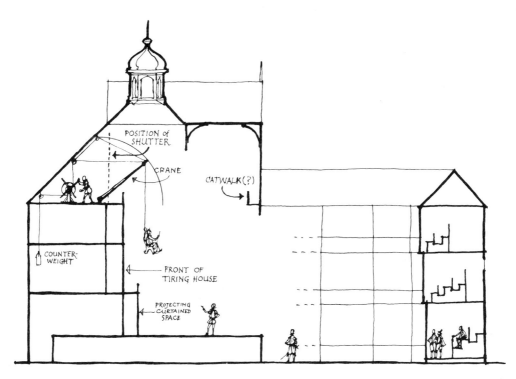

Diagrammatic section of the second Globe by C. Walter Hodges, showing the relative positions of lantern, tiring house and 'heavens'. From Shakespeare's Second Globe, *by permission of the author and the Oxford University Press.*

The second Globe Theatre on Bankside. This handsome building replaced Shakespeare's Globe after its burning down in 1613. Wencelas Hollar, the artist, worked from sketches he made on the spot, but in completing his work he probably exaggerated the onion shape of the dome above the lantern on the huts. This lantern itself, increasing the light to the rear of the stage or the tiring house, is a feature which shows how the King's Men improved their theatrical design with experience.

sixteen years have passed, and the whole tone of the play changes to light and lyrical pastoral, in which the rustic sheep-shearing makes idyllic setting for the love of the prince and the shepherdess; Autolycus the pedlar's deception of the shepherds provides an innocent background of mischief, and the tone is right for the restoration of Perdita to her true father and the spectacular revelation that her mother has not died after all.

In *The Tempest*, Shakespeare went a stage further in tackling the problem of tragic situations with comic resolutions. He swept the tragic element into the period before the opening of the play, and allowed Prospero to recount the events that led to his banishment on the magical island, permitting all the action to take place with Prospero firmly in control.

The play makes use of the technical possibilities of the indoor theatre by staging an elaborate masque. (*Cymbeline* had offered another). And 'a quaint device' the King's Men had developed was brought into play: evidently it was a table whose top was supported on a spindle, so that it could quickly be turned upside-down, concealing or changing what it bore. It would be used again in *The Two Noble Kinsmen* as a magical altar.

Prospero's farewell to his art, as he breaks his staff and prepares to return to govern Milan without the aid of magic, has often been described as Shakespeare's formal farewell to the theatre, as he prepared to go into retirement in Stratford. If this was his intention, he allowed the demands of his fellows to interrupt his provincial retreat as he certainly wrote his part of *Henry VIII* and probably his part of *The Two Noble Kinsmen* after

The Tempest. *The Two Noble Kinsmen*, mainly Fletcher's, is not especially interesting. It retells Chaucer's *Knight's Tale*, and the most characteristic moment in Shakespeare's contribution is a passage in which Palamon and Arcite debate whether they are right to fight for their king, Creon, whom they know to be a tyrant, against his enemy, Theseus, whom they know to be noble. The Shakespearean touch is that they decide that they should.

Henry VIII responded to another revival of dramatic fashion. Histories were again popular. The King's Men clearly wished to lay great stress upon the political documentary aspects of the reign: the title under which they were giving the play when the Globe burned down was *All Is True*.

But they also had a patriotic festive purpose. Although the play does not appear in the list of plays recorded as given at court for the occasion, it is almost unthinkable that this sequence of spectacles, with its climax in the rejoicings for the birth of Elizabeth, its prophecies of the greatness of her reign, and its carefully flattering prophecies of James, should not have been intended for court performance at the Princess Elizabeth's wedding. She was an extremely popular figure (as her brother Henry had been), and though her married life was darkened by the brevity of her husband's occupation of the throne of Bohemia, she is a pivotal figure in British royal genealogy. For it is through her that the Electors of Hanover derived their title to the English throne, and so through her that the present royal family claims its descent from James I, and ultimately, Henry VIII.

Back to Stratford

IN SHAKESPEARE's immediate family, the first note-worthy event after the deaths of John and Edmund was the marriage of Susanna in 1607. A young Bedfordshire man, John Hall, had brought his Cambridge and France medical training to Stratford in 1600, and seven years later he took Susanna to wife. Within eight-and-a-half months Shakespeare's first grandchild was born: a girl, Elizabeth. And, with the inevitable passage of generations, Elizabeth's great-grandmother died in the autumn.

Mary Arden is a shadowy figure. She had allowed her husband to manage her inheritance, not very successfully. She outlived him by six years. Her father's will seemed to suggest that she was one of the less quarrelsome women of his household. But she has become part of the Shakespeare myth because her maiden name derived from that lightly wooded area of Warwickshire, the Forest of Arden, and it is felt that her son, as sensitive to the associations of words as anyone speaking his language has ever been, must have felt a security about the name when he thus transcribed for peaceful pastoral purposes that Forest of the Ardennes which he found in Lodge's *Rosalynd*, the source of his *As You Like It*.

In the year of his granddaughter's birth and mother's death Shakespeare sued one John Addenbrooke for the repayment of a debt of £6. Nothing more is known about Addenbrooke, except that he had moved outside the jurisdiction of the Stratford courts, so that Shakespeare had to proceed against his surety, Thomas Horneby. Such proceedings were a commonplace part of the business life of the day. Another commonplace affair was Shakespeare's payment of his assessment for road repairs in Stratford in 1611.

Brother Gilbert the haberdasher had visited Stratford in 1602 to help with Shakespeare's purchase of land. In 1610 he was back again, witnessing a lease. Two years later he was dead, buried in Stratford in February 1612.

He was followed to the grave a year later by brother Richard Shakespeare, who had probably never left the town.

Now Shakespeare's only surviving sibling was his sister Joan, married since the late 1590s to William Hart the hatter, and still living in Henley Street, next to Hickock's Maidenhead Tavern. She was to outlive her remaining brother, and her children generated the line of collateral Shakespearean descendants. Her eldest son, William, became an actor like his uncle. He had no legitimate offspring, but the Restoration actor Charles Hart was reputed to be his bastard. If he was, then Shakespeare's grand-nephew was also reputed to have been Nell Gwynn's first lover, and to have trained her in acting. More respectably, the fifth descendant of Joan's youngest son, Michael became a furniture-maker in Tewkesbury, and established the line of Shakespeare-Harts surviving to the twentieth century.

Shakespeare's mother's home: Robert Arden's house at Wilmcote.

Michael Drayton, the Warwickshire poet who may have been visiting Shakespeare in Stratford when he contracted his final illness.

Rich John Combe died in January 1613 and was buried in Stratford church. He left Shakespeare £5, and collected an extraordinary place in his friend's legend. As a moneylender, his name was locally inserted in some traditional epitaph verses about the devil claiming a man who charged 10 per cent. Two unreliable late seventeenth-century accounts describe the verses as 'attached to' or erased into illegibility from his tomb. And an absurd tradition sprang up that Shakespeare had composed them.

The same year, Susanna Shakespeare encountered some trouble. Young John Lane, son of the owner of Alveston Manor at the western end of Clopton Bridge, put it about that Mistress Hall had 'been naught with Rafe Smith at John Palmer' and 'had running of the reins'. This latter phrase may imply that she contracted gonorrhea in consequence of her naughtiness, though more prudish scholars prefer to believe it means she ruled her husband.

The Halls were not pleased. Smith was a respectable haberdasher and hatter, related to Hamnet Sadler. Lane, on the other hand, was rather wild. He was to be labelled a drunkard in court in 1619, when he was charged with riot and libel against the Puritan Vicar of Stratford. He seems to have been an intemperate anti-puritan, and

John Hall has been suspected of puritanical tendencies. But in any case the Halls were not standing for his loose talk, and prosecuted him in the Worcester Consistory Court. The young man forfeited his case by failing to appear, and was excommunicated.

Public debate swept Stratford in 1613, as William Combe, old John's nephew, became the leading promoter of a scheme to enclose common land at Welcombe. Shakespeare's land holding and tithe farming gave him an interest in the proposal, but it engaged him far less than his relative Thomas Greene. Greene favoured the scheme, and hoped to profit by it. On the other hand, as town clerk he was expected to act on behalf of the Corporation which opposed it. In the event, he was as dilatory as he dared be, and rushed to and fro, trying to secure the acquiescence of his 'cousin Shakespeare' in the settlements the enclosers were offering interested parties.

Shakespeare seems to have given approval to the settlement without welcoming much discussion, and took no public part in the debate. In the end the Corporation successfully prevented the enclosure, and Combe was violently angry. When it was all over, Shakespeare casually told Greene's brother that he 'could not bear the enclosing of Welcombe'. He was not by our standards very old, but at fifty he may have been getting rather tired.

In 1614 the preacher of one of the Corporation's public sermons was mightily refreshed at New Place, where a quart of sack and a quart of claret were provided for him. Surely he should have been Falstaff's chaplain! (Actually the Chamberlain's laconic accounts are presumably misleading in their simplicity. The quantities, and the Corporation's acceptance of the expense, obviously suggest a small party given in honour of the visitor at a leading citizen's home).

At the very end of his life, Shakespeare saw his younger daughter settled at last. In February 1616, at the ripe age of thirty-one, Judith married Richard Quiney's third son Thomas. The groom was five years younger, and a month later was compelled to confess publicly to carnal intercourse with one Margaret Wheeler. The same month, his former mistress died in childbirth. This evidence of raffishness probably displeased his father-in-law. The will he made soon after carefully secured Judith's portion against her husband's extravagance. Nor was Shakespeare's misgiving misplaced. The young Quineys moved into a house at the corner of Bridge and High Streets (then called The Cage; now, inevitably, called after Judith Shakespeare). Within ten years Thomas was in trouble for selling adulterated wines and permitting tippling on the premises. Within twenty years, relatives took over the property to manage in trust for Judith and her children. And within forty, Quiney went to London and effectively deserted his wife.

The first sheet of Shakespeare's will.

But Shakespeare would not see all these things, any more than he would see the grandson who would be borne to him in November and bear his vanishing name, nor young Shakespeare Quiney's early death six months later. He himself was taken gravely ill in March of that year, 1616, and made his will.

A plausible tradition recorded by the Vicar of Stratford in the 1660s held that Shakespeare's illness followed 'a merry meeting' with Ben Jonson and Michael Drayton, at which Shakespeare may have drunk too hard, and in any case contracted the fever which soon carried him off. Drayton was certainly a Warwickshire man, known to visit Stratford from time to time, and indeed treated by John Hall a few years later. Ben Jonson, too, was quite capable of wandering around the country in search of congenial company. But it is only a tradition. We are on firm ground with the will Shakespeare dictated on 25 March and signed in a hand that grew increasingly weary as the three sheets were laid before him.

It was a revealing will. The oldest of his London colleagues were remembered, Burbage, Hemmings and Condell receiving 25s.8d apiece for mourning rings. Hamnet Sadler and three other Stratford men received similar gifts. William Combe's younger brother Thomas received his sword. William Walker, Shakespeare's godson, received 20s. in gold. The solicitor drafting the will and another executor received larger bequests; £10 went to the poor of the parish.

Then came the family. There were bequests of personal things: all Shakespeare's wearing apparel to his sister Joan; his broad silver gilt bowl to Judith, and the remainder of his plate to grand-daughter Elizabeth; the second-best bed with the furniture to Anne. There were small legacies: £150 to Judith, and a further £150 if she survived three years; £20 to Joan Hall and £5 apiece to her three sons. (Neither Shakespeare nor his lawyer could remember the name of the middle one, Thomas.) An important gift to Joan Hall was the use of her house in Henley Street at a twelve-penny annual rent for the rest of her life.

The real meat of the will was the bequest of New Place, the Henley Street property, the land outside Stratford, and the Blackfriars Gatehouse to Susanna. The property was carefully entailed on the 'heirs of the body' of Susanna; or, in default of her offspring surviving, of Judith. At the end of his life, Shakespeare wanted the fortune he had assembled to be held together in the hands of his senior descendants by primogeniture. Alas for human hopes, his line died out before the century was over, and his property wandered away through the Harts.

A month later he was dead. He was buried on 25 April, just a week after his brother-in-law Hart. He had been a prosperous and successful man, and his family saw to it that an appropriate memorial was erected in the church. And so we have the second guaranteed portrait of Shakespeare: the bust in the chancel of Holy Trinity church, Stratford.

It is as lifeless as the Droeshout engraving, yet like that picture, it satisfied those who knew the man. And, indeed, it is clearly the same man at a different stage of life. The face is fatter and a touch of complacency replaces the faint suggestion of melancholy hinted in Droeshout's face. The hair has receded across the head, and the man is distinctly bald, but still wears locks over his ears. They have a genteel curl, now, instead of the lank wave of his youth. The moustache is heavier, but still curls jauntily upwards, and the tuft below the lip has become a neatly trimmed chin beard. The fine nose is still apparent, and so too are the eyes, still seeming large almost to the point of prominence, yet set behind a prominent cheekbone and over heavy pouches. From the two definite portraits of Shakespeare we have no difficulty at all in listing his features, and as little sense of how he really looked as the sculptor who portrayed him busily writing on a cushion without looking at his hands had little sense of the appearance of a man composing poetry.

His true monument came seven years later. As early as 1619 it was clear that there was still a good market for printed copies of his plays, and the publisher William Jaggard started a surreptitious series of quarto editions, falsely dated and ascribed to other printers. But this was stopped, and the King's Men took the hint. Hemmings and Condell gathered up the scripts, prompt-books and manuscripts the company owned. Ralph Crane, the company's scrivener made fair copies of many of them, and a syndicate including publishers who had already been granted the title to some of the plays set Jaggard's printing house to work on the magnificent Folio volume of Shakespeare's plays. In 1623 it appeared. From then on, the word Shakespeare would, in the first instance, connote these plays.

The Man Shakespeare

WHAT KIND of a man was he? There is very little evidence upon which to base an assessment. No personal letters. One deposition in court, dealing with matters eight years earlier. Two formal dedicatory epistles. The sonnets. Fragmentary references by other people. A lot of business transactions. And finally, the plays, from which most speculative assessments of his character have begun. But the plays are works of fiction, and must be treated with caution. Let us leave them till last, and see what may be surmised from the factual evidence.

The recurrent feature of his dealings with other people seems to have been his extreme discretion; a cautious reserve which at times may almost have amounted to diffidence. He appears to have married young perforce. Tradition claims that he ran away from trouble to London. And then Chettle confirms that his manners were so gentle that an insult had to be retracted. There is caution apparent in his response to Quiney's request for a loan: Sturley's request has not been directly refused, yet Sturley doesn't seem very sure that he will actually see any money. In the Belott-Mountjoy case, Shakespeare's evidence neither helps nor hurts anyone. It makes a mockery of the proceedings, but it doesn't make Master Shakespeare any enemies. The Welcombe enclosures affair finds him as reserved as ever, saying nothing about his own opinions, despite pressure from cousin Greene; and finally telling a third party of the hostile attitude he would not reveal at the time.

A strange characteristic, this yielding nature. At its best it must have appeared as the perfect tact which led the Mountjoys to use him as their go-between with Stephen Belott. At its worst, it must have looked much less attractive. Can one believe that Abraham Sturley or Thomas Greene would ever have described William Shakespeare as a man whose word or support could be relied on?

This 'gentleness' of Shakespeare's is at its most extraordinary in the affairs chronicled in his sonnets. It almost surpasses belief that a man's response to being deceived by his mistress and his adored young friend should be to beg each, separately, to go on sparing him a morsel of their love. The only word I find fitting this is 'abject'. An unquarrelsome disposition, perhaps inherited by genetics or training from Mary Arden, was hardly an unmitigated blessing to Shakespeare.

To compensate for this lack of self-confidence, so extraordinary in an actor, Shakespeare seems to have been assiduous in cultivating the defences of worldly standing. He was quick to find a patron, and win the protection of 'divers of worship' once he attained prominence. His first determined action in his own behalf was the completion of his father's application for arms, which made him officially a 'Gentleman', and entitled him to be called 'Master'.

Thereafter he turned his attention to acquiring the security of property. Once again, his first purchase was one that brought him social standing: the largest house on the market in Stratford. And his major investments, land and tithes, were both gentlemanly, though not necessarily as profitable as 'knit stockings'. Sturley surely knew his man in holding out the gaining of good opinions as a bait to attract him into his tithe-buying consortium.

And at the end, when the goal of personal security was presumably achieved, how surprisingly mundane were his ambitions. Outside the realm of his fantasy, Shakespeare seems to have been a fairly unimaginative man, returning to his home town and hoping that his success would found a line of prosperous, armigerous burghers or petty gentry. Perhaps the complacency of the Stratford monument was the ultimately desirable goal: perhaps his sensitivity and dreadful awareness of not being greatly regarded by some of those he loved intensely meant that there was comparative ease and happiness in sinking back to a more stupid and unfeeling

The contents of the First Folio.

Full members of Shakespeare's company, the Lord Chamberlain's Men, later the King's men, as listed at the beginning of the First Folio. Not all, of course, were necessarily known to Shakespeare, several having joined the company after his retirement or death.

life of unthreatened comfort. Safe in his place within the social system, he clung to the membership of the King's Men that made him a Groom of the Royal Household even after he had retired.

When we look at the plays, we find the cautious conservatism of his business dealings and social aspirations confirmed. Of course, the plays also reveal intense sensitivity, profound insight into aspects of human nature, a deep love of the country, a delight in all kinds of sport, and oddities like a distaste for dogs (especially the abjectly devoted spaniel), or a peculiar fancy for theatrical situations involving boys dressed as girls dressed as boys.

But from start to finish we find an acceptance of the status quo, a respect for the established social order, and a distaste for change. From his earliest to his latest plays he is likely to give some character an opportunity to abuse the new-fangled fashions travellers bring in from abroad. When, after Essex's fall, a sullen note enters his work, the attack is turned upon ideals, rather than social

realities. *Love* is a delusion. *Heroism* is folly. *Victory* is a cheat. *Sex* is dirty. Never does he question the rightness of monarchical rule or hierarchical structure in society. Only in Lear's madness does he venture to attack the power of 'robes and furred gowns': and even then, he cautiously stays at the level of rather petty office holders.

Not until *The Tempest* did Shakespeare venture to write a play in which the socially senior member of the *dramatis personae* suffered a successful and justified challenge to his moral authority and control from a socially inferior but morally central hero. (Alonso is Prospero's overlord. And, of course, Richard III, Claudius and Macbeth as usurpers are not truly superiors.)

The truest description we can from our knowledge give of Shakespeare the man is, I believe, an unusually cautious conservative.

Acknowledgments to Illustrations

The paintings and other items illustrated in this book are reproduced by courtesy of their owners and are in the following collections: Earl Beauchamp, 436; Bodleian Library, Oxford 40, 42 left, 42 right, 46, 65, 124; British Library, London 15, 19 top, 30 left, 30 right, 71 top, 72, 108; British Museum, London 56 top; His Grace the Duke of Buccleuch and Queensberry 67 bottom, 100; The Masters, Fellows and Scholars of Corpus Christi College, Cambridge 57; County Record Office, Warwick 49; The Earl of Derby 26; Dover Library 78; Dulwich College Picture Gallery, London 60, 69, 101 bottom, 130 bottom, 136; F. H. M. Fitzroy Newdegate, 62; Fitzwilliam Museum, Cambridge 61 bottom; The Folger Shakespeare Library, Washington 93; Guildhall Library, London 56, 80 left, 121; Longleat House Library 33; The Marquess of Lothian 115; Lord Methuen, Corsham Court 64 bottom; National Galleries of Scotland, Edinburgh 54; National Portrait Gallery, London 29 top, 31, 61 top, 77, 80 right, 84, 85, 97, 99 top, 99 bottom, 104 top, 104 bottom, 105, 132; Nelson Gallery–Atkins Museum, Kansas City, Missouri 117 top; The Earl of Pembroke 51; Public Records Office, London 137; Shakespeare Birthplace Trust, Stratford-upon-Avon 14, 68, 140 left, 140 right; Shakespeare Birthplace Trust–Angus McBean 125, 130 top; Victoria and Albert Museum, London 8, 109 top.

Photographs
British Tourist Authority, London 9, 11, 13, 52 bottom, 131; A. C. Cooper, London 37 top, 51; Courtauld Institute of Art, London 33, 67 top; Anthony Crickmay, London 110, 111; Zoë Dominic Photography, London 86; J. R. Freeman, London 19 top, 20, 22 top left, 22 top right, 22 bottom, 25 right, 32, 36, 71 top; Hamlyn Group Picture Library 27, 91 top, 124 top, 141; Hamlyn Group Picture Library–Elsam, Mann and Cooper Ltd., Liverpool 26 bottom; Hamlyn Group Picture Library–J. R. Freeman and Co., London 108; Hamlyn Group Picture Library–F. Frith and Co, Reigate 135; Hamlyn Group Picture Library–John Wright Photography, Warwick 49, 112; C. Walter Hodges and Oxford University Press 73, 74, 89 top, 90–91, 109 bottom, 128 top, 133 top; Michael Holford, London 101 top; Mansell Collection, London 10 top, 16, 26 top, 29, 35, 47, 56 bottom, 79 top, 82 top, 82–83, 89 bottom, 95 top, 95 bottom, 98 top, 102, 106, 118 bottom, 120, 126, 133 bottom; National Portrait Gallery, London 41, 43 bottom, 44, 103, 115; The National Trust, London 18; M. Nimmo, A–Z Collection, Dorking 53; Pix Photos, Aylesbury 52 top; Radio Times Hulton Picture Library, London 12, 17, 21, 24, 34, 37 bottom, 45 top, 55, 78 top, 79 bottom, 81, 91 bottom, 92, 103 top, 114, 115 top, 118 top, 129 top, 129 bottom, 139 top; Ann Ronan Picture Library, Loughton 38; Royal Academy of Arts, London 62; Shakespeare Birthplace Trust, Stratford-upon-Avon 10 bottom, 137; Weidenfeld and Nicolson Archives, London 25 left, 43 top, 54, 64 bottom, 67 bottom, 78, 94, 100, 116, 117, 124 bottom.
In all other cases photographs were supplied by the owners of the items illustrated.

Index